F
Mast
From Simple
Pleasures to Mind-
Blowing Orgasms

Maree Stachel-Williamson

2nd Edition. Copyright © 2020

Maree Stachel-Williamson

ISBN: 978-0-473-54169-9

CONTENTS

Part Two: Physical stimulation techniques

<u>External stimulation techniques</u>

<u>Internal stimulation techniques</u>

<u>Miscellaneous stimulation techniques</u>

ACKNOWLEDGMENTS

I have an incredible gratitude for my husband, Jan. He always gives me an enormous amount of help and support while I write and edit my books. Thank you for listening to my ideas, being open to experimenting with me and being my main sounding board and editor. Jan, you are as always, amazing and appreciated.

Thank you to my Facebook friends who told me what they thought needed to be included in a book like this. Thank you to Laurinda-Lee for helping me edit the first edition of this book. Thanks to both Vicky Laird and Lindsay Tallman for their feedback on this edition and being open to my many "check this out" messages bombarding them with sex and masturbation information at any time of the day.

A massive thank you to Claudia Sobral, who drew some amazing illustrations for this edition and was wonderfully understanding about my specifics of how I wanted them to look. Claudia, there is no way I would have been able to draw the pelvis, clitoris and vulva as competently as you did.

And finally, thank you to Martha Kauppi for her wonderfully insightful training. You opened my eyes even further as to how we can claim our bodies and sexuality.

INTRODUCTION

Congratulations on the purchase of this book. It shows you care enough about your sexual pleasure to take action and learn how you can take ownership of your sexuality. Not only is masturbation a way to discover and explore your unique sexual self, it's also extremely good for your health. Way back in 1967, sex researcher and author R.E.L. Masters is said to have declared masturbation to be so good for us that if it didn't exist we would have to 'invent it'!

The exciting thing about this 2nd edition is that after listening to readers' feedback, I've added nearly 100 exercises and masturbation enhancement activities to try out as you read the book. This edition also has added scientific information – medical as well as psychological – about anatomy and arousal and covers additional toys as well as techniques for both mind and body. On top of that, I've compiled a handy self-exploration profile section near the end of the book so that as you experiment, you can document your preferences.

Building a clear understanding of your likes and dislikes will ultimately help you get more enjoyment out of masturbation, which is useful for your own playtime as well as being able to share your preferences with a sexual partner if you choose to do so.

Regardless of whether you are new to masturbation or exploring your sexuality afresh, you may also benefit from and enjoy the process of keeping a journal of your insights, emotional responses, beliefs and thoughts that come up while reading this book and doing the exercises.

This book is here to help open your eyes to new information, encourage you to try out new techniques and to approach masturbation with fun and curiosity.

Not everything in this book will appeal to you and that's totally fine, because I want to present you with a wide range of ideas and experiences that allow you to uncover more and more aspects of your sexuality. Each person is different and it is not for me or anyone else to tell you the depth and magnitude of your sexuality, desires and capacity for pleasure.

If you've been curious enough to wonder how high the rate of masturbation is among females, you're likely to have come across a varying range of statistics. Some studies show that 82% of females masturbate. Other studies, which have focused on the ages between 18 and 30 years, show the figures to be higher at 92%. Based on these studies, you would be right to assume that nearly every female you know masturbates in some form or another. However, other studies show much lower figures. The lowest I have come across was one specific to the United States, according to which apparently only 65% of females practice the art of self-pleasuring.

What to take of this? At least half, if not the majority of women masturbate. I think we're never going to get precise figures, because gathering completely honest data on sex is generally a tricky thing. Some people are just too plain shy or embarrassed to admit what they get up to – alone or with a partner.

Why do women masturbate?

The number one reported reason for females to masturbate is relief of sexual tension. Another common reason is that masturbation is something that women do while having sex with a partner to increase pleasure. Yet another reason behind masturbation is that it's a way to learn how to reach orgasm.

In this book, I'm going to do my best to convince you that you should be masturbating if you aren't already. You'll read about what happens in your body as you masturbate, become aroused and during an orgasm. And we'll be looking at orgasms themselves, the many types, the benefits of having them, and possible reasons why you might not have had one yet.

I take the stance that masturbation has a lot to do with learning to give and allow yourself pleasure. And that's why I'm going to outline numerous ways that you can masturbate so that you can explore and discover the most pleasurable ways for you.

If you are a complete newbie to the experience, this book will help you get some understanding of where or how you could start and what all the fuss is about. If you have been masturbating for years, my aim is to help you learn some new tricks, because even seasoned pleasurers can get into a rut or a habit.

Often people get into a routine with the way that they pleasure themselves or bring themselves to climax. I hope that with the help of this book, you'll understand the benefits of expanding your repertoire and, along the way, encounter many new ways to satisfy yourself.

This book is by no means a full exploration of all the existing techniques, but I cover techniques that focus on external and internal stimulation as well as those that involve your mind. You'll discover ways that you can pleasure yourself using just your hands, various options that incorporate sex toys like a vibrator, and numerous other methods. And, because masturbation is an act of self-pleasure, I also address body acceptance, working through psychological challenges and ways in which you can embrace your sexual self on a daily basis.

Why I wrote this book

As a teenager I had vaginismus. It's a condition in which the vaginal muscles clench together making sex very painful and sometimes impossible (as was the case for me). I was extremely fortunate that it only affected one relationship, but the experience gave me an appreciation of other ways of experiencing sexual satisfaction aside from penetration.

In addition to my early experience of painful sex, I've encountered some interesting thoughts and beliefs about sexuality and what is supposedly okay or not – according to my various boyfriends – over the years. This led me to read and research quite extensively into the topic so I could discover and claim my sexuality as part of my individuality.

When I had vaginismus, my boyfriend and I became quite focused on just trying to have sexual intercourse and I didn't really care about whether I had an orgasm or not. Although he wanted to 'give me' an orgasm, it really wasn't that important to me, because I enjoyed being touched by him and could get extremely aroused through feeling his hands on my body and mine on his. It was just the intercourse that was missing for me.

(If you're interested you can read more about my personal story in my ebook – Stop Painful Sex: Healing Vaginismus. A Step-by-Step Guide.)

In subsequent relationships, sexual intercourse became physically possible and the orgasm topic came up again.

Often there were times when my boyfriend at the time would try to give me an orgasm. Although the attention was great, their constant attempts distracted me from simply enjoying the intimacy. Over time, I became indifferent to orgasms and claimed I didn't care. The reality was that I just found their obsession stressful. However, after a number of years, I realized that I had become curious about orgasms myself and thus decided to take it into my own hands. To avoid creating any feelings of pressure, I decided to simply play and explore rather than actively focus on trying to orgasm.

Self-pleasuring allowed me to finally explore my sexuality in peace without any pressure from anyone else. First I was able to discover the type of touch I liked. I explored with sex toys and experienced my first orgasm and multiple orgasms. Eventually I was able to build the courage to give myself an orgasm while with a partner and go on to learn how to climax during sexual intercourse. It has been through self-pleasuring that I have been able to explore many avenues of my sexuality in my own way and time. Taking charge the way I did has immensely improved my sex life and made me feel empowered.

My personal journey and the stories I hear from other women have led me to the understanding that masturbation or self-pleasuring (whatever you want to call it) can be an extremely important element to a woman's expression of herself. It is a demonstration of independence, self-reliance and pure pleasure. It is an act of claiming your sensuality and sexuality and it is the right of every woman (whether in a relationship or not) to experience and enjoy sexual pleasure.

How to read this book:

The best way to read this book is playfully. I urge women to approach sexual exploration with a sense of curiosity and playfulness and it is with this same attitude

I recommend you read this book. You don't have to start at the beginning and read word for word through to the end. Have a look at the table of contents and go straight to the parts you are most interested in. From there, jump from section to section to your heart's delight. Alternatively, for a more comprehensive experience, feel free to read from start to finish.

Disclaimer:

Hopefully, buying a book about masturbation means that you're open-minded and ready to learn about all sorts of aspects and possibilities of sexual enjoyment. I haven't held back on any topic that I have felt is necessary or useful to include in this book. If something seems too challenging as a topic, of course feel free to skip to another section.

PART ONE: LEARNING ABOUT YOUR BODY, MASTURBATION AND ORGASMS

1. What is masturbation?

Masturbation is basically just touching yourself for pleasure in a sexual way. Some people focus on their genitals while others touch and stimulate other areas of their body at the same time. Masturbation can be done with just your hands or you might incorporate sex toys. Orgasm is optional but common. Some people fantasize at the same time as touching themselves, some people watch porn, while others focus purely on the sensations in their body. Masturbation may be thought of as a purely physical act by some, and yet many consider it a more holistic act, which includes aspects of their emotional, mental and spiritual self.

The key thing is that masturbation (aka self-pleasuring) is normal, common, safe and healthy. It is each individual's right to choose if they want to masturbate, when they want to masturbate and how they want to masturbate. It is only considered a problem when it gets in the way of someone's life. An example of this could be if it negatively affects the ability to be sexually intimate with a partner or if it is repetitively used as a distracting behavior to avoid facing emotional challenges or commitments in daily life. For some women, masturbation is in conflict with religious and societal beliefs they grew up with. This can lead to feelings of guilt and shame and it can therefore be helpful to work through these emotions with a trusted therapist.

Generally speaking, however, for the majority of people masturbation is a pleasurable expression of sexuality, self-care and love, which brings health benefits including stress relief, a boost to self-awareness and confidence in knowing what you like.

2. Benefits of masturbation and orgasms

Reason #1: Less stress

In the journal article: *It's Happiness and Relief and Release*, masturbation is identified as something that can be used as a stress relief tool after a challenging day. And the reason why is clear: Bringing yourself to a climax, whether alone or with a partner, helps reduce physical and mental stress, can release physical tension and lead to feelings of calm and relaxation. In an interview with magazine Spiegel, singer Billie Eilish talks about how she regularly uses it, even multiple times a day, as a coping mechanism and stress reliever.

Reason #2: Use it or lose it

Orgasms help keep our vaginal tissues healthy, moist and supple. This is, because regular orgasms increase blood flow in the pelvic area and stimulate the vagina's natural self-lubrication process. In addition, just like any muscle, with age a woman's vagina will atrophy and lose its elasticity if it is not penetrated for a long period of time. This can make intercourse as well as gynecological exams uncomfortable or even painful. Penetration (whether by finger, penis, vibrator, dildo or dilator) and activation of your pelvic muscles (such as during orgasm or by doing Kegel exercises) help keep your vaginal muscles and tissues healthy. This is one reason why you might choose to include vaginal penetration in your masturbation options.

If you are going through menopause and noticing the effects of hormonal changes such as thinning of the skin of the vulva and vagina and/or a decrease in vaginal lubrication, then consider following 'The Vaginal Renewal ® Program' by A Woman's Touch. It is an online, free to download program with a step-by-step plan you can do in your own home to recondition the health, strength and flexibility of the vaginal skin and tissue, increase moisture, and heal old scar tissue. A Woman's Touch also has programs and recommendations for pelvic floor muscles that need strengthening or relaxing (both are important). I recommend them a lot, because their information is reliable and made generously available to the public.

Reason #3: Know your body

Sexologists have discovered that women who have sexual issues as adults have often missed out on the natural, early self-exploration phase in their childhood and youth. This can be the result of negative messages from caregivers, religion or the wider community about masturbation. In some cases it can be a result of early trauma or abuse. Even though this sounds like doom and gloom, the wonderful news is, it's never too late to start playing catch-up with self-exploration or challenge old beliefs that you learned while growing up.

According to extensive studies, 61% of women say they always or usually can orgasm by masturbating and 29% report they always orgasm during sex with a partner. Many sex therapists believe that most women have the ability to be able to orgasm even if they haven't yet. There are some health conditions which may hinder an experience of orgasm (Dr Ruth Westheimer et al mention diabetes and severe depression as examples). Most of the time, however, failure to reach orgasm is a result of simply not knowing the right technique that works for you or due to psychological challenges or both. For many women, especially young ones, it can also be a case of not having the confidence to communicate to their partner what they would like or need in order to get more aroused. Therefore, masturbating plays an important role, because it helps women get to know their body and what turns them on.

Reason #4: Improve your sex life and keep it alive

Masturbation sensitizes the body to sensual and erotic touch. It increases both your body's responsiveness to and interest in sex. The more you stimulate your nerves with pleasurable touch, the more the nerves grow. This has the positive effect of increasing your sensations and enjoyment.

If you are in a relationship, masturbating won't reduce the amount of sex you want to have with your partner, it'll more likely increase it. This is good news for women who are frustrated with a low libido and want to do something about it.

Reason #5: Pain relief

Orgasms lower pain. The South Illinois School of Medicine did research on the effect of orgasms on migraines and found that out of 52 migraine sufferers, eight reported their migraine completely gone after an orgasm and another 16 reported considerable relief. Women who regularly have an orgasm also have a higher pain threshold, concludes research at Rutgers University. Orgasms can also help relieve menstrual cramps.

Reason #6: Improve your health and live longer

The hormone DHEA increases in the body shortly before orgasm which enhances focus and desire as well as possibly spiking dopamine levels at the same time. DHEA, which is sometimes referred to as the 'anti-aging hormone,' is thought to improve brain function, protect the immune system, repair body tissues, lower cholesterol and encourage healthy skin.

Research has also shown a connection between orgasms, prevention of heart attacks, and a decrease in the risk of breast cancer. Orgasms have been shown to play a role in helping prevent endometriosis. They may also help bring a baby to term in pregnancy. Furthermore, the increased muscle tone of the pelvic floor muscles (the muscles that support the uterus, bladder, small intestine and rectum) is beneficial for bladder control, more intense orgasms and greater enjoyment during sexual intercourse.

Reason #7: Natural feel good drugs

Having an orgasm releases 'feel good' chemicals (endorphins) into your bloodstream. Endorphins give us a natural high, help block or reduce pain, and generally make us feel good. People often talk about the 'high' they get from exercise and it is the endorphins that play the role there as well.

And you know how energetic and happy people feel at the start of a relationship? This is partly because the body releases high levels of the hormone PEA (phenylethylamine) at this time. PEA is a natural amphetamine (stimulant) which gives us a feeling of giddiness and excitement.

Interestingly, there is a connection between depression and low levels of this hormone in the body. The good thing is you don't have to keep seeking out new relationships to get this natural high. It is also released every time you experience an orgasm. How awesome is that!

Reason #8: The ultimate in safe sex

By practicing self-love through masturbation, you effortlessly protect yourself against the numerous risks of partner sex including sexually transmitted infections, pregnancy and other possible risks that come with sexual encounters with others.

This is a compelling reason for people of all ages to feel at ease with and to enjoy masturbation. However, this also raises an interesting dilemma for some people: To act out a fantasy in real life or not. Regardless of your decision, it's an unfortunate truth that many people who do decide to bring a fantasy to life say it was not as 'hot' as they expected it to be. A bad experience in real life can even reduce the fantasy's power to turn you on in the future. One option therefore is to keep your fantasies as daydreams in which you are both the director and actor; ensuring the fantasy stays super hot, you keep full control over the story line and the actions of any other characters... and you're guaranteed safe sex.

Reason #9: Self-reliance

Masturbating helps you learn to take charge of your own sexual satisfaction. Imagine you didn't know how to cook food. You would be in a situation of either having to order out or eat convenience foods or rely on others to cook for you. And in that situation you may never be able to get the meal that you really crave – that you would be able to make for yourself if only you knew how. It's the same with self-pleasuring. Learning how to do this is a gift to yourself, a gift of being able to satisfy yourself exactly the way that you love the most. You become self-reliant and have another way of being able to express self-love and self-care.

Reason #10: Stronger connection with your partner

Many women who have not yet experienced an orgasm during sex or haven't been fully enjoying the act of sex, realize that masturbation allows them to discover and explore their sensuality and sexual self in their own way and in their own time. The knowledge gained through self-pleasuring can greatly enhance a woman's positive sexual experience during sex with a partner.

Learning how to have an orgasm is also beneficial for the emotional connection with your partner. When you have an orgasm, your brain releases oxytocin. This is a natural chemical that promotes feelings of attachment and bonding. Once you know how to give yourself an orgasm, you can incorporate this during sex, which will increase the feeling of closeness with your partner. And knowing how you give yourself an orgasm means you are better equipped to be able to teach your partner your preferred style of touch as well. Oxytocin also gets released during kissing and touching, so you don't miss out during orgasm-free but nevertheless intimacy-rich moments.

Reason #11: Sweet dreams

The physical relief and relaxation that occurs as a result of an orgasm can help you get to sleep. Some women use masturbation to help them in this way when having a restless night or as part of their bedtime routine.

Reason #12: Simultaneous orgasms with your partner

Masturbation is an easy way for you to learn what turns you on and which movements bring you to a climax. You don't need to masturbate in order to figure this out and you could instead explore with the help of a partner. However, the feedback process between two people is a lot more complicated than with just yourself. It can be done, you just need even more patience.

Like any skill, controlling your arousal and orgasms is something you can get better at with time. Regularly masturbating women often report that they can give themselves an orgasm quicker than in the past, because they know exactly what they like.

Combine your ability to orgasm easily with a partner who has also practiced self-control and awareness and you can stretch out and enhance the experiences of intimacy with the knowledge that you can orgasm at the same time (if that is something you aspire to).

3. What is an orgasm – How to recognize when you're having one

What is an orgasm? Scientifically speaking, an orgasm is a physiological response to a continuous and high level of arousal. In plain English, it's the climax and release of sexual tension and arousal.

Orgasms and arousal require multiple body systems to be healthy and functioning well. They involve the heart and healthy blood circulation throughout the body. The body needs to be able to activate both the parasympathetic and sympathetic nervous system and hold them in balance for both arousal and release. Our skin needs to be healthy, both strong and flexible for sustained touch as well as having healthy nerves to feel the stimulation in an enjoyable way. Our hormones play a role as well, so any medications that affect them or big hormonal changes (e.g. pregnancy and menopause) will have an effect on arousal and orgasm. And we need to have strong and flexible pelvic floor muscles, because a large part of an orgasm is the contractions of those muscles.

There are slight differences between women due to our unique bodies. Each orgasm is also nuanced according to the situation, stimulation, accompanying emotions and thoughts. Generally speaking though, an orgasm can last anything from a few seconds up to minutes. The length of the orgasmic experience also depends on the type of stimulation leading up to it and whether it is experienced as a single or multiple orgasms.

There are different ways to reach an orgasm. The obvious way is through clitoral stimulation which is how the majority of women have one. In fact, 70% of women require an average of 30 minutes of direct clitoral stimulation to orgasm. As you will learn later, if you didn't already know, the clitoris goes a lot deeper than just the little nub that we see on the outside, so internal stimulation can be part of the sex play to orgasm. But really think about this fact: *70% of women require an average of 30 minutes of direct clitoral touch to reach orgasm.* Remember, when we talk about averages, that means there is a continuum of experience. Some women need much less time and some need a lot more. There is a big range of normal, therefore part of masturbation and learning to give ourselves pleasure is understanding our own body and working with it.

So forget those movie scenes where the woman has an intense orgasm after just a few deep thrusts of a penis. That's not real life. Remember that. That said, within the other 30% of women there are some interesting alternative pathways to orgasm. For example, an orgasm can happen in our sleep, as vaginal lubrication is a natural part of the sleep phase in which we dream. It can also happen through thought alone (although just a measly 2% of women have been found to have this ability). It can also happen through non-genital touch, for example of breasts and other areas of the body. This is especially interesting for people who have become paralyzed or lost feelings in parts of their body. Learning to create a neural pathway and thus connecting sexual pleasure with non-genital touch can be part of rebuilding and maintaining a sexual self.

If you have never had an orgasm and have started experimenting either by yourself or with a partner, you will benefit from mindfully noticing the physical sensations, emotions and thoughts as you play and explore. There are definite signs that you can look for that will let you know you are having an orgasm. As you continue exploring and experimenting with different types of touch, you can start to get a feel for what you find most pleasurable and what increases your arousal. With time and patience you'll also get to the point where you will have the option to bring yourself towards orgasm when you choose to have one.

How to recognize an orgasm in yourself?

Just as all women are unique and have individual sexual 'tastes' in terms of what turns them on, we all have our own unique orgasmic experience. An orgasm can range from being felt as just a quiver of sensation to a powerful, breathtaking event. Regardless of your experience up until now, it's useful to let go of any preconceived ideas you have about what an orgasm 'should' look, sound or feel like that you may have picked up from comments by lovers, family, friends, movies, books or porn.

The common experiences of an orgasm are bodily convulsions and contractions, which are followed by a sense of physical and emotional release and relaxation. During an orgasm, your body will have an increase in muscle tension, breathing rate, as well as heart rate and blood pressure. During an orgasm, there is a sense of having reached the height of arousal; a state of being in bliss. For many, an orgasm is often felt as a full body experience, which includes an emotional aspect as well as the physical sensations. These typically intense feelings reach a climax and then rapidly fade unless you continue stimulation in order to have multiple orgasms.

The interesting thing about multiple orgasms is that often people think that only women can have them, because when men ejaculate there is a hormonal release, which creates what's called a refractory period. In order to come again, they need to wait for that refractory period to pass. The refractory period can last from a few minutes, an hour, several hours, a day or more. The length in time depends on things like health and age. However, in men, orgasm and ejaculation are actually two separate events with three seconds in between them. With practice, men can learn to control their arousal levels so that they experience the orgasm and not the ejaculation. Those who learn this are often able to then also learn how to have multiple orgasms without such a long refractory period. If you know of a male who would be interested in learning this, the book *The Multi-Orgasmic Man: Sexual Secrets Every Man should Know* by Mantak Chia is a good recommendation. The author also has a multi-orgasmic book for women if you are interested in learning from Taoist sexuality teachings.

Back to the female body! *In The New Joy of Sex*, the ability to experience multiple orgasms is described as a matter of the "subtle mix of physiology, mood, culture, upbringing and having the man (or woman) she wants."

When experiencing multiple orgasms, each one can be slightly different in its physical and emotional intensity or the physical location of where the energy is released and focused. Multiple orgasms can be experienced either as a continuous string of orgasms with no clear big peak or as consecutive orgasms with a short pause and rebuild between each one. It is likely that more women could experience multiple orgasms if they put the time into exploring their arousal and orgasms more and noticed what happens when they practice continuing stimulation in various ways.

4. Common reasons for not having had an orgasm yet

Why have I not had an orgasm yet? The possible reasons are wide ranging. Just because you have enjoyable sex doesn't mean that you will automatically have an orgasm. And just because you or your partner stimulate your clitoris, it doesn't mean it is necessarily enough or the right type of touch to produce an orgasm either. If you are curious or even confused why you haven't had an orgasm yet, consider whether any of the following apply to you.

Some possible reasons to consider:

– The stimulation hasn't been in the right place, for long enough or in the right way for you.

– You have never masturbated and therefore have no practice in turning yourself on and bringing yourself to climax.

– When masturbating you give up too soon.

– You have a particular idea of what arousal and orgasms 'should' be like and your experience doesn't match that – therefore you've labeled your experiences a failure.

– With little or no masturbation history or history of direct stimulation from partners, your clitoris needs stronger stimulation to 'wake up'.

– You have a history of unskilled partners and limited knowledge from your own exploration.

– You tune out or dissociate during sex as well as masturbation due to past trauma.

– Being vulnerable isn't something you're okay with, even with yourself.

– Clitoral stimulation is either too soft and not stimulating enough, or too hard and direct, leading to pain rather than pleasure.

– You are always stressed out and thinking about other stuff like work or family commitments during sex or masturbation.

– You have beliefs and feelings of shame, embarrassment or anxiety associated with masturbation, orgasms, or sexuality, which are getting in the way of your carefree and enjoyable exploration.

– Masturbation and sex is always a rushed affair or you expect you should orgasm within a certain time frame – you don't give yourself enough time.

– You've always tried to have an orgasm through penetration alone instead of including direct clitoral stimulation.

– Sex and masturbation is goal focused. You only masturbate with the aim of trying to orgasm rather than relishing in the pleasure you're giving yourself.

– The vibrator isn't strong enough.

– You take medication that affects one or more of the following: libido (desire), lubrication, arousal or the ability to orgasm. Some culprits might be medication for blood pressure reduction, allergies, depression, anxiety and pain. If in doubt, talk to your medical doctor who will be able to discuss alternatives.

If you are taking prescribed medication, do not stop or alter your dosage. Instead, have a discussion with your doctor about your concerns and the side effects. It may be possible to be prescribed an alternative, which does not affect you in the same way. You can simply say to them: "I think that I am having sexual side effects from my medication. Is there a medication that does the same thing that doesn't have any sexual side effects?" Be prepared to explain the specific side effects you have been experiencing since taking the medication such as lowered interest in sex and/or less lubrication or other arousal response plus anything else. You can help advocate for yourself by being precise about what has changed.

If you haven't had an orgasm yet: In the book, *The Multi-Orgasmic Woman*, the authors point out that most women who have never had an orgasm can learn to with the right information and motivation. I like to think of it as one of many skills we can learn. And just as with any other skill, if we never put the time and effort into learning and exploring how our body gets aroused and can orgasm, how can we expect it to happen? The wonderful thing is that this particular skill requires giving and feeling pleasure within yourself. When you think of it as undertaking a journey of learning to enhance your experience of pleasure, it sounds like something worth your time and effort, doesn't it? Depending on how you approach it, enriching your experience and knowledge about your body can be something to look forward to regardless of your experience up until now.

Take any pressure off yourself and adopt a mindset of playing – with curiosity and aiming for pleasure, regardless of how aroused you are or how close or far you think you are to orgasm. Prioritize your sexuality, your exploration and expression by making time to do the exercises in this book regularly.

5. Myth busters – Common beliefs and misconceptions

Masturbation is for singles only – Studies on masturbation show the majority of women who masturbate regularly are in long term relationships. It

28

doesn't mean that the sex has dried up in those relationships. Those who masturbate regularly also show as being the most fulfilled in their sex lives. So if your partner ever questions the benefit of your pleasuring yourself, you can tell them it's for their benefit as well!

If I haven't had an orgasm yet, then I obviously can't – This one I've heard particularly from older women who start to question their sex lives and sexual satisfaction after getting divorced and leaving a long marriage. When I've questioned them about this belief, I typically discovered that a) they haven't put much or any effort into exploring their sexuality and how to pleasure themselves and b) their husbands didn't know how to please them either. For many women, orgasms don't just happen without effort, so if it is important to you to have an orgasm, perhaps it's time to start the journey?

I'm too old – You don't have to limit yourself, because of a number. Just as you are never too old to eat chocolate cake with your hands, go skinny dipping or grow your hair long, you are never too old to masturbate or start playing and exploring your sexuality. Whether a teenager or a gray haired retiree, your body and soul will appreciate your giving yourself some loving attention. A beautiful example of this was highlighted by sexuality consultant for women, Pamela Madsen, when she invited her 93-year-old mother Roslyn to attend one of her sexuality retreats. Pamela quoted her mother's feedback several days into the course on her Instagram account: "I found out that my sexual eternal flame has not gone out. Inside I am the same sensual being that I always was." "If older people did this, they would find out that their aches and pains would go away." "It's so sad that people don't know about sexological bodywork, some people would spend their whole lives stuffing their sexuality down. At 93, I am no longer ever going to do that."

Its dirty/sinful/naughty/God doesn't approve – I'm not going to preach to anyone about what is right or

29

wrong morally. Sometimes religious beliefs can clash quite strongly with sexual practices and you need to figure out what sits right with you. For Christians, you might want to take a deeper look into the topic. Masturbation isn't specifically mentioned in the bible let alone forbidden and any interpretation of it as a sin is an application of another part of the Scripture regarding sexuality.

I'll go blind – I'm kind of including this belief as a bit of a joke. In the past, this was one of the things told to small children to scare the living daylights out of them and hopefully stop them from giving themselves sexual pleasure, which the adults were uncomfortable about. Rest assured, masturbation is a natural part of a child's development and helps build confidence and understanding of their body.

I'll get addicted to masturbation – There is still officially no such thing as 'sex addiction' despite what the media wants you to think. There is the diagnosis of hypersexual disorder, but it goes far beyond simply desiring sexual satisfaction or masturbation. Some people have a high libido and enjoy masturbating daily and that's fine, others might masturbate once every now and then and that's fine too. It's only an issue if it creates problems in other areas of your life. What can happen is that masturbation might increase your overall sex drive and pleasure receptors. At the end of the day, your body will let you know if you have had enough simply by becoming too sensitive to further touch.

I'll get addicted to my vibrator – While you can't get 'addicted' to your vibrator in the clinical sense of the word, you can get used to it in a way that makes reaching climax with other methods harder. But that isn't a vibrator-only concern. It's something for everyone to keep in mind no matter what genitals you have. When you have an orgasm by any method, your brain creates a neural pathway connecting that method with your orgasm. Subsequent orgasms by that same method strengthen the pathway. Over time if you only use one method to orgasm, other methods will become harder. Not impossible, but more difficult.

Therefore, switch it up. When you masturbate, try different techniques and add variation to how you increase arousal and the method you are using at the point of climax. Don't just rely on any one toy or technique. Learn how to orgasm using your fingers and in different positions. You might want to consider whether your techniques are compatible with being with a partner. The more you switch it up, the more neural pathways, ie. ways to orgasm, you'll have.

If I haven't been able to orgasm yet, there must be something wrong with me – Ask yourself the following: How much effort have I put into learning how to self-pleasure? How often have I masturbated and how many different techniques have I tried? Do I understand female anatomy with regards to sexual arousal? Is it possible that I have given up too soon? Or is it possible that I've been taking it so seriously that stress and anxiety have been getting in the way? For many women, their lack of orgasm thus far is due to one or more of the above reasons.

On the other hand some experts on the topic say that inability to reach orgasm is a serious health concern and one to talk to your health professional about. Of particular concern would be if you have been able to orgasm previously and no longer can even when doing your tried and true techniques. Worth considering is whether you are taking any medications that hinder arousal and orgasm and discuss alternatives with your doctor. Noting any other changes and talking them through with a sex positive health professional is worth considering especially if you have been through a significant hormonal event such as pregnancy or menopause or have had surgery in the pelvic area. Weak pelvic floor muscles might also mean that you don't feel your orgasms even if you have them. If you think that could be the case, then you could benefit from seeing a pelvic floor physiotherapist.

It may be something physical, it may be psychological, it may have to do with your medication or it may be that you just haven't learned how to yet. If it's important to you, get a professional's opinion so you know what you can do about it. And if you are one of the women who report a satisfying sex life without any orgasms that's fine too.

No-one talks about it, therefore no-one does it – Well this one just isn't true. Statistics prove that. Additionally, the general consensus is that due to women's embarrassment about masturbation (which leads to this kind of belief) reported figures are lower than the reality.

Even if it were the case that none of your friends masturbated, why should that mean that you need to miss out as well?

That area is for my partner to touch... not me – I've heard this a couple of times, and it's a belief that severely limits a woman's ability to discover and take ownership of her body and sexuality. I guess if you really had this belief, then you wouldn't be reading a book on masturbation. However, if this belief lingers in the background for you and you would like to change it, you could explore where it comes from and replace it with a new belief about your body that is more positive.

If I masturbate, it must mean that my partner isn't satisfying me or I must be with the wrong person – The truth is that you having the ability to please yourself sexually does not mean that your partner is unable to. The two aren't necessarily related.

Over your lifetime there will probably be times when you want an orgasm and you are alone or you want sexual relief and your partner isn't in the mood. Rather than create a whole lot of negative interpretations about what that means about you, your partner or your relationship, you can instead satisfy yourself if you know how. Being able to masturbate has no connection with the satisfaction of a relationship and can even lead to hot sexual experiences together (because of what you know about yourself and can teach your partner). With the pressure off your partner, their arousal can be triggered by your sexual confidence and expression.

When it comes to relationships where the sex has become unsatisfying, you have the choice of ignoring it and eventually letting it become stale and even die out completely. Or you can choose to address your sex life and explore new options together as well as alone. A woman who masturbates is likely to be more confident in her sexuality and able to give their partner some tips and techniques on what turns them on. So rather than being in a position of helplessness, masturbation and the knowledge that comes from it can be an act of empowerment.

And remember, neither masturbation nor sex is all about having an orgasm. So if you are unsatisfied, it's possibly a cue to put more effort into the relationship in general.

Masturbation needs to be done a certain way and I don't know how – Where did you get this idea? If you have heard about masturbation in books, online or from porn and got the impression that there is a 'right' way to do it, then here's some great news: That's not the case! Just as sex isn't all about penetration, masturbation isn't all about the technique or the orgasm. Think about masturbation as self-massage. The aim might be different depending on the day or the time or where you are in your monthly cycle. Regardless of the day, do it to give yourself an experience of pleasure, relaxation, sexual release or part of expressing self-love and acceptance.

6. Understanding arousal and the arousal process

Anatomy of arousal – Which parts play what role?

Let's get specific with anatomy. While you might already know a lot about it, some information will hopefully be new and helpful in understanding your body and some of the biology behind female sexual arousal. Either way, I encourage you to give these areas of your body some curious attention and explore what you enjoy and experience in each area. Even though I will use and explain various 'spots' like the G-spot, U-spot and A-spot, the thing I want you to remember is that at the end of the day it's all just various tissues and nerves that create pleasure when stimulated. Nerves, in particular, branch out through the whole genital area resulting in a high level of sensitivity.

So while it can be an easy way to remember particular 'spots', notice what you personally enjoy in the moment, because how each individual creates sexual pleasure will be unique to them. If you find that you're not enjoying or getting aroused from stimulation in one area, relax, and move to somewhere else that does feel good.

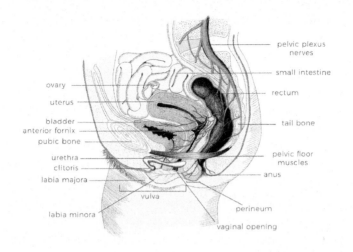

Image above: A cross section of the pelvis

Vulva

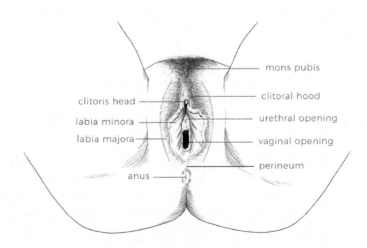

The vulva is the outer female genitalia. It includes the mons pubis, clitoral hood and head, outer and inner lips (labia), urethral and vaginal opening, perineum and some experts include the anus.

There is huge variation in what vulvas look like. Everyone is different and all shapes, colors and lengths are normal. A modern and common misconception is to think that the type of vulva seen on mainstream porn sites is the only normal and all women's bodies should look that way. This is simply incorrect and a belief that can be very damaging psychologically. Be aware that mainstream porn models are typically chosen for a particular body type and specific traits, which are not representative of the vast range in the general population (as opposed to those in ethically produced and feminist porn).

Three things in porn create misunderstanding again and again: Very small inner labia, little to no pubic hair and uniform skin tone. Firstly, inner and outer labia come in lots of sizes and lengths. Remember, porn models are often chosen, because they have small inner labia or they've had surgery to look that way. Secondly, pubic hair is a completely natural occurrence on your whole genital area including around your anus. Removing hair doesn't improve hygiene and actually leaving your pubes 'au naturel' plays a role in providing a barrier against bacteria from entering your vagina. In contrast to this, irritated skin from hair removal puts you more at risk of infections, including STI's. Regardless of risks and benefits, choosing to trim or remove your pubic hair is a personal choice and not something you should feel you should or shouldn't do if you don't want to. Lastly the skin tone of a vulva (including labia, perineum and anus) comes in a variety of shades with some areas much darker than the tone of the rest of your body. If you've seen a vulva with uniform, pale skin tone in porn, it's likely due to skin bleaching. Mainstream porn is the culprit for creating a false idea of what women look like down there.

I encourage you to become familiar with your unique, beautiful vulva. Access pictures of vulvas online or in books so you (and your partner, if they need some education) can get a positive reality check. Make it a goal to accept and love yourself and your vulva along with the pleasure it can give you.

Clitoris

The clitoris is the only organ in the human body that exists solely for pleasure. And what a lot of pleasure it can bring! No wonder really, as it contains approximately 8,000 sensory nerve fibers, which is more than anywhere else in the body. You might have noticed, I left out most of those thousands of nerves and nerve endings from the pelvis diagram so that you could still see the other parts!

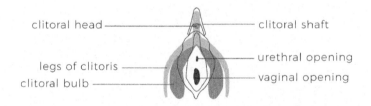

Many people still think the clitoris is just the little ball-shaped tip at the top of the labia. However, this little tip is only a very small part of the whole. The clitoris has a tip (sometimes called a head, glans or bud), shaft, two bulbs (corpus spongiosum) and two legs (corpora cavernosa or crura). The bulbs and legs run along each side of the vaginal entrance underneath the labia and can be stimulated from inside and out. The length from top to bottom is approximately 3.5 inches. The clitoris is made of the same type of erectile tissue as the penis and also has very sensitive nerve endings. During arousal the whole clitoral body becomes engorged as blood flow increases to the area. A natural ebb and flow of engorgement (swelling) during sexual play is also normal and healthy. There are many ways of stimulating the clitoris. It can be touched directly by pulling back the hood. This is its most sensitive part. The head can also be stimulated indirectly through the hood. The legs and bulbs can be stimulated through the tissue of the vulva and labia where the legs connect with the pubic arch, and through the tissue at the outside of the vaginal entrance. Internally, the legs and bulbs can also be stimulated such as during penetration or insertion of fingers rubbing past or pressing up against the internal parts of the engorged clitoris.

Some women report their clitoral head is too sensitive to touch after orgasm and for some it can be too sensitive directly before an orgasm. There is also a high chance of over-stimulation if directly stimulated for a long time or with too much pressure, which may then lead to discomfort. One way around this is to build up your arousal and sexual tension by including stimulation of other areas of the body and vulva rather than focusing only on the clitoral head. This also gives you a greater chance of being able to have subsequent orgasms (by not overstimulating the head of the clitoris in the lead up to the first orgasm).

Labia majora and labia minora (aka outer lips and inner lips)

Each woman's labia (aka vaginal lips) are unique and come in different shapes and sizes. Some inner lips can be bigger than the outer lips, which is why the majora and minora terms can cause confusion and just like breasts, the left and right side typically don't look the same. It is normal and natural for pubic hair to grow on the outer labia but typically not on the inner labia. Labia are body parts that many woman become self-conscious about due to incorrect and unhelpful ideas of what labia

look like. If you need some reassurance, check out bo,
like A Celebration of Vulva Diversity by The Vulv
Gallery, or look at the online photo gallery at
www.labialibrary.org.au which gives a photographic idea
of just some of the various forms labia can take. In some
cases, women get labiaplasty to alter the labia for
cosmetic purposes (which is very different to needing it
for health reasons). However, someone who had this
surgery to reduce the size of her inner labia told me she
regretted it, because she experienced a reduction in sexual
pleasure from touch to this area after the surgery. This
was possibly due to scar tissue or the reduction in her
labia, which contain nerves that provide pleasure.

Stimulation of the labia can be direct by stroking, gentle
squeezing, spreading and tugging. Tugging on the inner
labia gently and indirectly stimulates the clitoris due to
their close proximity and connecting tissue. Rubbing
and pressing against the labia also indirectly stimulates
the clitoral bulbs and legs underneath.

Urethra

The urethra is the tube that carries urine from the
bladder out of the body. From the outside only the
opening is visible. Its location is higher towards the belly
button than the vaginal opening. Rubbing against the
opening of the urethra can be pleasurable for some
women and not for others.

Paraurethral tissue – aka G-spot

This is where things start to get really interesting. You've
heard of the G-spot, right? Have you heard it called the
paraurethral tissue before? I'm guessing not. The
paraurethral tissue wraps around the urethra and it is this
tissue that is being stimulated when reaching inside the
vagina an inch or two and tapping or rubbing towards
the front of the body. Some women find G-spot
stimulation enjoyable and some don't, so experiment for

stimulation of this area can result in female
(aka squirting), which is a mix of extremely
̲..̲c̲u sterile urine and paraurethral fluid ejaculated out
of the urethra. Some females do experience ejaculation
and some don't and both are normal. If you want to
explore ejaculation you can compare the difference
between pushing down on your pelvic floor muscles
during G-spot stimulation when highly aroused or
pulling up and in (like doing a Kegel exercise) and
activating your pelvic floor muscles. Pushing down on
these muscles is more likely to lead to ejaculation than
pulling in, but pulling in also creates a lot of pleasure for
some women and contributes to a strengthened muscle
tone.

Hypogastric nerve plexus

Starting from the spinal cord reaching down behind the
bladder and other pelvic organs and branching all the
way down to the vaginal opening, this is a dense
collection of nerves that can bring very pleasurable
sensations when stimulated. Just like the paraurethral
tissue, very few people are aware of or understand the
role these nerves play in sexual enjoyment. It can be a
more reliable source of pleasure than the paraurethral
tissue (G-spot).

You may have heard of the A-spot? Way back in 1993, a
Malaysian physician, Chua Chee Ann, M.D., researched
how repeated gentle stroking of the area deep inside the
vagina and towards the belly button quickly resulted in
77.5% of study participants experiencing "copious"
vaginal lubrication and 39.1 percent experiencing
orgasm. He called it the A-spot (referring to the
biological name: anterior fornix) but what he had
actually studied and 'discovered' was essentially an area
where the hypogastric nerve network ran past. As with
the G-spot, this area can be stimulated with long and

curved vibrators and can result in deep orgasms. Alternatively you can experiment with deeply inserting your index finger into the vagina and tapping forward towards the front of the body.

Vaginal opening and vagina

Being touched on the skin around the opening of the vagina is very pleasurable for many women. Most vaginal sensations are felt in the first third of the vagina making the opening a worthwhile spot to explore with different types of stimulation. The stretchy opening can be penetrated, if desired, by a tampon, finger, toy or penis.

As outlined with the clitoris, paraurethral tissue and hypogastric nerve plexus, penetration of the vagina can stimulate many pleasurable areas, erectile tissues and nerves. Penetration can also include in front of and behind the cervix deep inside the vagina. The front (anterior fornix) doesn't have much space and isn't accommodating of thick penetration but touch or vibration here in front of the cervix stimulates the part of the hypogastric nerve plexus Dr Ann called the A-spot. In contrast, the area behind the cervix (the posterior fornix) opens with arousal and is very stretchy. It is the space where an erect penis or toy can deeply penetrate into if desired, because the average vagina is shorter than the average penis. As with the area in front of the cervix, the posterior fornix is also close to parts of the hypogastric nerve plexus.

Cervix

This is the opening to the uterus deep inside the vagina. Some women find touch around the cervix pleasurable and others don't. Explore what works for you.

U-spot

People seem to like to give labels to areas and this is
another example of that. I've come across the U-spot
being referred to as the space running between the labia
from clitoral head to the opening of urethra (medically
known as the vulval vestibule). I've also seen it restricted
to just the area to either side of and directly above the
urethral opening. Because women's bodies are different
and the distance from the vaginal opening and urethra is
unique to each body, I'm going to suggest you think of
the space between the labia from vaginal opening to
clitoral head when you think of the U-spot, because this
whole area is pleasurable to touch for most women
especially when lubricated and lightly stroked with a
finger or licked from bottom to top. But sometimes I
might simply refer to this as the skin between your labia
or lips, or specify it as the area around the urethral
opening. At the end of the day, don't worry about
whether you're within the official boundaries of the U-
spot or not. As always: just follow the pleasure!

Perineum

The area between the vaginal opening and the anus is
called the perineum. The tissue and skin here is stretchy
and the absence of bone structure allows for penetration
as well as giving birth vaginally. This is another area that
can feel pleasurable to be touched. Try light strokes with
a lubricated finger.

If this area becomes damaged due to surgery or tearing
during birth, healing can be helped through self-
administered treatments such as ice packs and gentle
massage of the forming scar tissue. Ask advice from a
female health professional on how to do this. The
perineum can also become inflexible due to a reduction
in estrogen. Following the free online Vaginal Renewal
® Program from A Woman's Touch may be beneficial in
this case.

Anus

The skin around the anus as well as inside the rectum is a source of pleasure for many people due to the many nerve endings there. Because the anal passage doesn't produce its own lubrication, penetration of any kind requires lubrication and often gentle and patient opening of the sphincter muscles if it is to be comfortable. If you experience pain it is likely to be a result of muscles that haven't relaxed, lack of lubrication or both.

Keep in mind that anal stimulation isn't pleasurable for all. Like any sex act, it is normal and healthy to have a preference about whether you want to engage in anal stimulation or not.

Also, it is important to pay attention to hygiene. Ensure any fingers and toys used around this area are carefully washed before bringing into contact with your vaginal and urethral opening to minimize the chance of introducing bacteria and getting an infection.

Pelvic floor muscles

This hammock-like group of thirteen muscles surround the pelvic organs and hold them in place. The PC (pubococcygeus) muscle, that you may have heard of when learning Kegel exercises, is just one of these muscles that we contract and release when doing Kegels. Having muscles that are strong as well as flexible and able to relax is important for bowel and bladder health (holding it in as well as releasing) as well as penetration (the muscles need to relax in order to allow vaginal penetration).

Simply speaking, orgasms are the rhythmic contraction of the pelvic floor muscles, which in itself stimulates the clitoris. This explains why many women find exercising these muscles pleasurable. Strong muscles also mean strong orgasms. However if you have only exercised tightening these muscles and not relaxing them you might experience difficulties such as painful penetration later in life. Weak muscles after childbirth or simply due to aging processes can lead to unintentional loss of urine or stool as well as a weakened sensation of orgasms. Difficulties with the pelvic floor muscles can be helped by a pelvic floor physical therapist. If you have rigid pelvic floor muscles, a pelvic floor physical therapist can help you release tension, and in the case of weakened muscles, teach you how to regain strength.

Erogenous zones

An erogenous zone is any area in the body that creates a sexual response when stimulated. So most of the areas described above can also be called erogenous zones. The interesting thing is erogenous zones aren't limited to our genitals. You know this if you've ever felt turned on by the touch of your breasts, side of the neck or brush of your inner thigh.

Some people with physical disabilities report that their bodies adapt by simply creating new erogenous zones in places that previously weren't sensitive in a sexual way. Their erogenous zones simply 'relocate' to other areas. How amazing is that! These new erogenous zones become more sensitive and allow for extraordinary ways to reach orgasm. The body creating new erogenous zones after the loss of the old ones shows how biologically important it must be that human beings experience sexual feelings. Our bodies are truly impressive!

Taking the time to touch and be touched all over your body will reveal your many erogenous zones. You may find certain areas of your body create internal bliss when touched. Why not take the time to explore them all.

Time to play:

Exploring your erogenous zones

Set aside at least 15 minutes for this full body exploration. In a comfortable setting, clothed or unclothed (wearing light clothes if at all), guide your touch over every inch of your skin's surface. You might like to start with the soles of your feet and work your way up or start with your head and work your way down.

Play with varied touch and notice the different sensations you experience when drawing soft lines with your fingertips versus a full palm caress. Notice the difference between caresses and pressing down with some pressure.

As you do this exercise, pay attention to the following: Which are the areas where you sink into bliss? Which areas do you want to linger on with your touch? Where are you ticklish? And can those ticklish areas also provide enjoyment if caressed slowly and gently?

Jot down in your sexual exploration notes the areas that you want to remember as feeling particularly good for future reference.

Partner variation: 15 minutes each way

A lot can be learned by doing this exercise as a couple. Follow the same directions as you did in your solo exploration, but this time notice what the difference is when the touch is made by a loving partner and when you don't necessarily know where their hand is going to move next.

As your partner touches you, feel free to share during the process what feels good or not.

Note: Although you might be tempted, do not linger at

the obvious spots of sexual pleasure. Remember this is an exercise in exploring touch across the whole body!

The sexual arousal cycle

There are numerous reasons why it can be useful to understand the general stages a female body goes through during arousal. The main one, in my opinion is to be able to have the arousal phases in mind as you learn and become familiar with how your body responds in each of these stages when alone and/or with a partner. The more you learn about your body's response as well as your likes and dislikes at each stage, the easier it becomes to repeat your favorite moves and sequences as well as know what to ask for from a partner, so that sex becomes even sexier rather than a guessing game.

There are five main phases reported in the female arousal process (also referred to as the 'human response cycle'). These are the desire phase, excitement phase, plateau phase, orgasmic phase and recovery phase. I've added the rebuild phase to the illustration in this book to incorporate the additional option of multiple orgasms. Notice how the diagram illustrates the intensity of arousal as it builds with each phase. Understanding this process is a good starting point for getting familiar with what's actually going on in your body. As the line illustrates, arousal builds with pleasurable and sustained stimulation.

By the way, it's important for you to realize that what I'm showing you is a simplified model for ease of learning. It doesn't reflect the nuanced experience of real life. Generally we don't experience an actual separation of the phases leading up to an orgasm and subsequent recovery. Instead it is more likely to feel like an overlapping experience of growing arousal with possible and even likely dips. Many women experience arousal as a fluid path; increasing or decreasing, depending on the stimulation as well as their emotions and thoughts. Secondly, all sorts of things can get in the way of arousal and it's not actually a straight forward process at all. You might jump from one phase back to another due to external circumstances such as a phone call, hearing someone else in the next room or noticing the time and realizing you're late for something and you need to stop. It might not be until later in the day or another day entirely that you reignite the arousal process and continue. You might even purposefully reduce or stop touch for a moment; easing right off before building back up again through to orgasm. This is a technique called edging that can be used to create a more intense orgasm (more on that in Part four: Enhancing Pleasure & Strength of Orgasms).

There are other personal circumstances that might also hinder the arousal process from occurring as easily as the model suggests. Some medications (e.g. SSRI antidepressants) and even some hormonal birth control methods can hinder the body's response either through affecting hormone levels, libido, mood, lubrication or the ability to orgasm. Menopausal and post menopausal women often experience a change in the tone of their pelvic floor muscles and also require more time for their body to produce lubrication. So what might have worked in the past doesn't get the same result and needs renewed experimentation and possibly support from a pelvic floor physiotherapist. Furthermore, if you are stressed and thinking about what your body looks like or about work or feeling anxious about whether you can give yourself an orgasm or not, it is also highly likely you will not reach orgasm.

In addition, not all women experience orgasm every time they masturbate or are intimate with someone. An orgasm is not compulsory. And some don't orgasm at all. Whether because they haven't learned how or because they choose to or due to other circumstances. It is perfectly okay to enjoy sexual exploration and pleasurable feelings up to a certain intensity of arousal and then stop. Just as it is perfectly okay to continue stimulation beyond orgasm to create multiple orgasms. When we stop stimulation at any phase of arousal (with or without an orgasm) our body naturally goes into the recovery phase. Examples of this are: Masturbating without the desire for an orgasm, enjoying making out with someone and indulging in sexual pleasure without taking it to the orgasm stage.

Therefore, being aware of the arousal phases can be a useful element of understanding your body, and at the same time it can be just as useful to let go of theory and focus on enjoying the sensations. So without further ado – the phases:

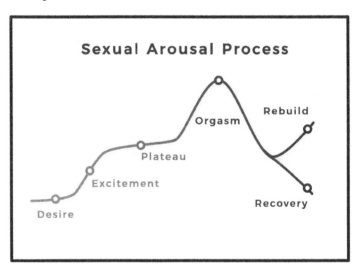

Sexual Arousal Process

Desire phase

The desire phase starts when you are in some way stimulated. The stimulation can come via any of the senses; not just touch, but also sight, sound, smell, and taste. The initial stimulation will be something that is erotically pleasing for you, whether it's part of an actual situation, such as being touched a certain way, seeing a naked body, reading erotic literature, watching porn, smelling your partner's scent, tasting a romantic and delicious meal, or mental creations such as sexual fantasies in your mind, thoughts or memories that spark arousal and desire.

When it comes to partner sex, some women's desire for sexual contact might not be based purely on sexual desire but also draws from a longing or need to connect emotionally with a partner and feel loved, accepted, or emotionally close. There are also two different modes of how we might experience desire. Some people experience 'Spontaneous Desire'. What that means is that they can be going about their day and out of nowhere notice they're turned on and would like to have sex or masturbate. Others have 'Responsive Desire' (more common in females). In this mode, desire isn't triggered until sexual stimulation has started in some way. The important thing to understand with this is that no matter how you operate, both modes are normal and healthy. It also helps to remember this if you operate from a responsive mode and your partner from a spontaneous mode. People often fall into the trap of incorrectly thinking something is wrong with them. There isn't. It's just that you're operating from different modes.

That's why in some relationships a couple might miss out on sex completely, if they wait until the person with a responsive desire system feels sexually aroused. The sexual touch itself may be the first trigger for desire for them. And this may then lead to wanting more. And if arousal doesn't continue to build, then as with every couple, there are numerous ways to continue intimacy or caring connection, such as shared massage or naked cuddling. Being willing to share intimacy is enough to start. This is what has led some sex therapists to encourage couples to initiate sexual touch even if they aren't necessarily 'in the mood' or to schedule it into their diaries. By making the commitment to prioritize sexual intimacy, that part of the relationship can still be sustained and cherished without relying on spontaneous desire.

When it comes to masturbation, knowing what your desire mode is and how you can stoke it is also important. Is your mode responsive or spontaneous desire? This will affect how you instigate self-touch and whether it is something that comes to you as an idea and desire all by itself or whether you have to make a date with yourself and give yourself time to warm up to feeling desire in any way.

Therefore, in this stage, whether alone or with a partner, touch is about sparking desire, sexual interest and a willingness to explore and play. Once triggered, it can feel like a hunger that wants to be satiated or an itch that wants to be scratched. Many women prefer gentle movements at this stage, which may or may not include genital contact.

Time to play:

– Read erotic stories, listen to or watch sexy movies or ethically produced porn and give time to yourself regularly to indulge in your fantasies.

– Remember and replay memories of hot sex and sexual play with yourself or with a partner or when you were feeling particularly sexy in the past.

– Send your partner (or yourself) a description of what you would like to experience or what you are remembering.

– Connect with your sexuality with a loving and body focused sensual meditation.

– Try long, slow, soft and teasing caresses as you aim to spark your desire.

– Set and prepare the scene. Address and remove anything that will distract you or prevent you from giving in to pleasure.

– Glide over your inner thighs with light fingertips or a flat palm.

– Rub scented oil onto your skin with a self-massage while listening to music you find arousing before moving on to more direct sexual touch.

– Gently cup and massage your breasts. Draw soft circles around your nipples.

– Connect with your internal sensations by pulsing your pelvic floor muscles.

– Stroke up and down your labia with underwear still on.

– Circle, press and caress the clitoral head with light touch.

– You may want to avoid direct contact with your clitoris or vaginal entrance at this initial stage unless you have already been triggered into feeling sexual by thoughts or sensations.

– Not ready for touch yet? Trigger feelings of desire by reading some erotica and daydream being one of the characters in the story, luxuriate in a bubble bath with candles and enjoy the feeling of the water caressing your skin. Recall your sexiest memories and play them over in your mind, do some exercise that tunes you in with your sexy side, be it dancing in a sexy outfit or feeling your muscles while working out.

– Teasing movements: Regardless of the direction of movement, play with coming close to touching your clitoris, but brush past it.

Excitement phase (warmup)

The excitement phase is the body and mind warming up sexually to the thoughts and feelings of desire. In this phase, heart rate and blood pressure rise and there is an increase in muscular tension in the body. In light-skinned women, there can be a noticeable flushing of the skin around the chest area. Nipples may become erect and as blood flow increases to body tissues, the clitoris, labia, and nipples swell and become darker. The vagina also starts to moisten as it secretes lubricating fluids.

The length of this stage can vary according to the amount and effectiveness of the stimulation as well as other contributing factors such as health, age and medication use.

In contrast to males who get the clear signal of a penile erection as a sign of arousal, females require more self-awareness to notice signals of their arousal. It is possible that a female can start to become physically aroused without realizing it consciously or actually feeling mentally or emotionally aroused or interested in sexual touch. This disconnect between mind and body has been shown in laboratory research where a control group of women, given no instructions, reported a lower awareness of arousal after viewing erotic material compared to other groups who were instructed to notice signs of arousal. These included vaginal lubrication, pelvic warmth, muscular tension, increase in heart rate, nipple erection and breast swelling. The groups instructed to pay attention to their physical response showed a high correlation between their self-reports and the actual physical reactions.

This gives us females a very good reason to increase

awareness and knowledge about our bodies and practice bringing our attention into our present sensory experience through mindfulness practice and Sensate Focus exercises (both included later in this book). Please note, however, that when it comes to sex with another person, only you are the ultimate judge of whether you are turned on and interested in sex. Just because someone says you're wet, doesn't mean you should ignore other signs within yourself about whether you want to proceed or not. And it is okay to say no and follow your gut if you do not feel comfortable.

During the excitement phase, masturbation feels satisfying for many when it becomes increasingly more direct. Aim to sustain and build on the established interest and hone in on areas and movements that increase pleasure.

Time to play:

– Dip a finger into the vaginal opening and drawing the wetness up between your labia with an occasional passing beside or around the clitoris.

– With a moist finger (your own vaginal fluid, saliva or lubricant), tease yourself using circular movements that gently caress your clitoris and circle your vaginal opening.

– Spread the inner labia with outward strokes.

– Hold a vibrator at the vaginal opening and insert it gently as you get more and more turned on.

– Whatever movements or techniques you use, you can enhance your arousal by tuning into the growing warmth inside your vagina and drawing out the pleasure by mixing it up; following slow, indulgent motions with faster strokes and then back to slow again.

– Increase awareness and connection with your internal

sensations by softly clenching and releasing your internal muscles at the same time as touching yourself or using a toy.

– Stimulate your body in multiple ways at the same time. Increase speed and intensity as your arousal builds.

– Explore short and fast as well as long and slow movements.

Plateau phase (build up and approach)

This is an extension of the excitement phase with a sustained level of pleasure as you get into a rhythm and pattern of movement that is creating the most enjoyment for you. If you continue stimulation at this point and allow yourself to stay mentally connected with your sexual arousal, then sexual tension will increase with a heightened desire for a release as you approach and then experience orgasm. For women who are learning to build up to having an orgasm or choose not to have one, this period of continued pleasure can continue as long as they wish or until they get too sensitive for further touch.

As arousal rises past the excitement phase, the vulva becomes more swollen and the clitoris, if it hasn't already, becomes erect and exposed from the hooded skin around it. The area around the nipple, called the areola, also swells. Your preferences of stimulation in this phase will be unique as there is a lot of variation between women.

Some ancient practices such as Tantric Sex teach how to prolong this phase, which can lead to more intense orgasms and the ability to quickly become re-aroused and experience further orgasms. However, if you are interested in enhancing and extending your orgasms as well as becoming multi-orgasmic you don't have to study Tantric practices to gain this benefit (more on this later).

For many people, learning how to simply relax into and enjoy this phase without performance pressure can be a very rewarding experience. You can learn how to do this by practicing mindfulness and allowing yourself to relax and focus on pleasure during masturbation. And in the case of having sex with a partner, indulging in this phase, connecting with your body and your partner (without the goal of trying to make each other have an orgasm) can be extremely beneficial in enhancing the bond and emotional intimacy.

It is common to have very specific requirements in the moments just before orgasm in terms of what type of touch or stimulation will work best. Near the end of this plateau phase is when it becomes clear to you that you are about to come or that an orgasm is within reach. Generally, women report needing consistency at this point. This means continuing whatever movement you are doing; either exactly the same or with only a slight increase in pressure and speed. For some, any deviation in movement at this point can cause them to 'lose' the orgasm and have to essentially start again.

Time to play:

– Explore different levels of pressure from light, gliding strokes, to firm massaging touch.

– Notice the location where you get the most pleasure such as around the clitoris and hood, the vaginal opening, inside the vagina or around and inside the anus.

– In your exploration, play with different variations of touch such as strokes (up and down, side to side, circular), vibrations, pressing, flicking, squeezing, tapping and pulsing to find what works best for you and makes you orgasm.

– If you orgasm easily, explore drawing this phase out and learn to luxuriate in your full-body experience.

– If you are however discovering that you need a lot of stimulation and time before having an orgasm and would like to quicken things up, use a vibrator and explore stimulating your clitoris internally as well as externally. Vibrators are known to cut the time to orgasm in half.

– Mix up or combine clitoral touch with G- or A-spot stimulation with a curved vibrator or finger.

– Allow yourself to breathe deeply, move around and moan.

– As the pleasurable tension and warmth builds continue the movements or stimulation that is giving the most pleasure.

– Focus all of your attention on your bodily sensations. Engage all of your senses in the experience.

– Play with stopping and restarting stimulation (edging) if you want to delay or intensify your orgasm.

Orgasm phase

During orgasm, the uterus and lower third of the vagina contract in waves. You may also experience waves of contractions or jolts throughout your body. Each orgasm will be unique in its length and level of intensity depending on many factors including mood, amount of time taken in the build up, hormones, technique, and whether it is the first or subsequent orgasm.

You will find similarities and differences between your orgasms. Research shows that the majority of women (70%) reach this climactic phase through some kind of clitoral stimulation. If you haven't already, I'm going to encourage you to explore touch even during an orgasm. Notice the difference between when you stop touch near the start, middle or end of an orgasm versus when you continue touch. What happens for you?

Time to play:

– As your orgasm pulsates through your body, play with continuing the same type and intensity of stimulation on the same spot.

– Alter the location of stimulation after the peak of orgasm. If you are touching your clitoris, shift focus to your vaginal opening, inner lips, or to more indirect touch. Notice how this affects your orgasm. Does it increase or decrease the level of pleasure for you?

– Draw the experience out by increasing or decreasing pressure, slowing down or speeding up. As you try each of these over time, you may come to prefer particular variations over others.

– After the peak of orgasm try adding or stopping penetration.

– Note, that these are all ways in which women have discovered how to extend the length of their orgasm. For some, more touch and pressure leads to more intensity, while for others, reducing stimulation increases focus and awareness of their bodily sensations.

– Remember that everyone's different. Experiment and find out what feels good for you! Continuing touch during orgasm is one way in which you can progress through to multiple or subsequent orgasms. Practice without pressure and give yourself time to build this new skill.

Next time you have an orgasm, pay close attention to the experience and see if you can answer the following questions:

– Where in your body did you feel the sensations?

– What metaphor fits your experience? For example, was

57

it like a wave washing over you, a series of jolts of energy, going over a roller coaster track, like a tightening pressure with a sudden warm release or something else?

– What emotion or emotions do you feel at the moment right before, during and immediately after your orgasm?

– What was the movement that you were doing when you had an orgasm? For example, firm strokes along one side of the clitoris, circling the clitoris, vibrations against the G-spot, using a particular toy?

– Were there any images or fantasies that helped you orgasm?

– Notice how orgasms can differ for you.

– Does the time of your monthly cycle noticeably affect the intensity of your orgasm?

Recovery phase

After orgasm or stopping stimulation without an orgasm, the muscles begin to relax and you will experience a sense of overall relaxation unless you continue touch in some way. Immediately after your orgasm, you may experience a gentle continuation of energy flowing through your body as the orgasm subsides. Heart rate and blood pressure begin to come down from their elevated levels. Any flushing of the skin disappears and the engorged tissues in the labia and clitoris begin to return to their normal state. Nipples and areolas also return to normal. The clitoris retreats back to its original position and can be extremely sensitive at this point for some women.

In general, if stimulation is discontinued at this point then the body will completely return to its normal, unaroused state within around 30 minutes.

Time to play:

– Instead of immediately getting up and moving around or starting to think about other things, stay with a conscious awareness of your body as it drifts back to neutral.

– Notice and follow your breathing and tune into feeling sensations and energy throughout your body. Pay attention to how your vaginal muscles feel, the rise and fall of your breath and your rapid heart beat as it starts slowing down again.

– Observe your emotions and thoughts. Float along with any enjoyable thoughts and also observe if any unhelpful, limiting or negative thoughts or feelings come up. These might be a result of past experiences or negative beliefs about yourself or your body. If this is the case, just take note of them without judgment. If you find stressful thoughts or emotions returning again and again after sex or orgasm, you might benefit from discussing and exploring them further with a trained therapist.

– Whether you have had an orgasm or not, choosing to be mindful and connected with your body after a time of self-pleasuring can also be a source of pleasure in itself.

– Support a body-mind connection by placing a hand on your chest and one on your belly. Tune into your heartbeat and your breath flowing in and out.

– Send love and gratitude for the pleasure you have just experienced through your body. Cup your vulva and breathe deeply as you feel the inner waves reside.

Rebuild phase

Although less than 50% of women report having multiple orgasms, it can be fun exploring what happens if you either continue touch throughout your orgasm, or take a short break (a few seconds through to a few minutes) and then resume touch.

If you continue stimulation, then you might experience a second orgasm immediately. Alternatively, you might feel an ebbing back to the plateau phase before the arousal rebuilds to another orgasm. You may wish to spend more time languishing in the pleasure; purposefully dragging it out before you make yourself reach another climax. Or you may simply enjoy continuing touch without experiencing another orgasm. The clitoris typically gets more sensitive during and after orgasm, so you may have to focus your strokes elsewhere or simply become more indirect by stimulating the clitoris through the hood or labia. Remember, explore what feels good for you!

Time to play:

– Continue tuning in with your bodily sensations as you resume or continue touch. Listen to your body and be playful and flexible in your movements, because what works one day may not work another day.

– As you orgasm, try continuing the exact same movements in precisely the same way for a second orgasm.

– If the clitoral head is too sensitive to touch directly after orgasm, make a V with two fingers and rub it from each side of the hood or return to some of the other movements you liked earlier in your build up.

– Explore penetration and massaging of the G-spot while caressing the clitoris to broaden the range of sensations again after climax.

– Keep bringing your attention back to the body if your mind wanders. This is a useful tip for all stages of arousal and during sexual experiences in general. That said, it is especially useful when you explore rebuilding for multiple orgasms initially, because you may need to be patient as you learn what kind of touch and movements increase the sexual tension again for you.

– Treat yourself as a new person in subsequent build ups to orgasm. What worked previously may not work now depending on your sensitivity.

– Try adjusting pressure (light, medium, firm), style of motion (stroking, pressing, pulsating, flicking), direction (circles, up and down, side to side, on spot) and rhythm (consistent pattern, irregular timing, missing a beat/passing over a spot every now and then).

Accelerators and brakes – The dual control model

Have you ever wondered what causes sex and masturbation experiences to sometimes feel easy to enjoy while at other times requiring effort or giving you a sense of unease? Janssen and Bancroft at the Kinsey Institute came up with the Dual Control Model, which explains an important aspect of the arousal process. Let me explain it to you, because I think it is useful to understand how you operate for the benefit of both masturbation and partner sex.

The Dual Control Model explains how, when it comes to sexual arousal, there are two systems at play: The Excitation System (what turns you on) and the Inhibition System (what turns you off). For simplicity's sake let's use a driving metaphor and call them the accelerator and brake. Things that act as accelerators turn us on and move us forward in arousal. Brakes turn us off and literally put the brake on our arousal and interest in continuing.

61

Everyone has a unique sensitivity regarding each of these systems. Your accelerator system can be sensitive, which means lots of things spark arousal, or you you can have an insensitive system, which means hardly anything sparks arousal. The brake system operates the same way with very sensitive at one end of the scale where lots of things turn you off and stop arousal. At the other end of the scale, someone with an insensitive brake has few things that stop arousal or turn them off.

An important thing to understand about this model is that the two systems operate independently.

Therefore, you can have a sensitive accelerator and brake (easily turned on and lots of things turn you off).

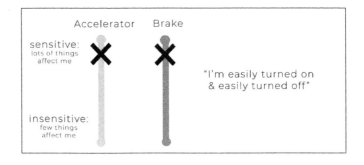

An insensitive accelerator and brake (where it's hard to get turned on but once aroused hardly anything throws you off).

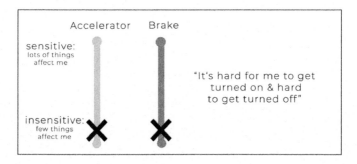

A sensitive accelerator and insensitive brake (lots of things turn you on, and hardly anything pushes the brake).

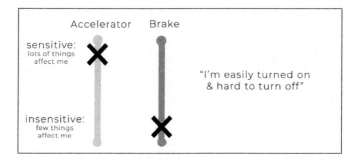

An insensitive accelerator and sensitive brake (it's hard to get turned on and lots of things hit the brake).

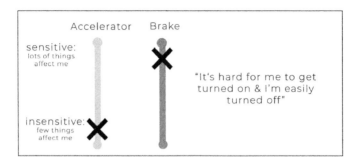

Or you could be somewhere in the middle of the range for either system.

Still with me? So now, thinking about yourself, how easily is it for you to get aroused? Some people have a long list of things that can push the button for arousal. These can include: I'm home alone, that person looks hot, I've got my sexy top on, the kids are in bed, I smell good, you smell good, it's my birthday, you're touching me the way I like, the sun is on my skin, my new toy has arrived, I feel good in my body... and so on. Someone with a highly sensitive accelerator might only need one of these things to be happening in order for them to be triggered into arousal while at the other end of the scale someone with an insensitive system would need many things to align before they feel aroused. Write a list down of your accelerators (for partner sex as well as masturbation if you like or just masturbation). Take a guess at where you think you are on the scale, at one end of very sensitive or very insensitive or somewhere in the middle?

Now think about your brake system for a moment. Do you lose connection with arousal and have an internal brake with many things or just a few? Things like: the kids might interrupt, someone might hear me, this is risky, I feel fat, I think masturbation is a sin, I feel bored, there's a bad smell, your breath smells, that hurts, we don't have a condom, I'm full, I'm tired, I don't know if I'm doing this right. Again, if you have a very insensitive brake none of this will bother you, and if you have a very sensitive brake, you'll find that lots of things stop you from continuing. Now write a list of the brakes you can identify for yourself and ask yourself where you would place yourself on the brake system scale, very sensitive or insensitive or somewhere in the middle?

What does all of this have to do with masturbation? And how can you benefit from knowing this when it comes to partner sex? The important thing with our dual arousal system, is that if you have things hitting the brakes, you have to address them first, *before* pressing on the accelerator can make a difference. There's no point hitting all your arousal buttons if you haven't sorted out your brakes. That means, identify and start working on any unhelpful and restricting beliefs and emotions about your body, sexuality and sex, and anything that gets in the way of feeling free to enjoy exploring. Also become aware of what you need to do to set the scene for yourself so that you can relax and let go. This applies to any self-loving sessions as well as sex with a partner. Knowing yourself in this way is just another way that you are able to take more and more control over your sexual experiences with self-care and understanding.

Forms of orgasms

There seems to be a lot of confusion about orgasms. On the one hand, pioneering sex researchers Masters and Johnson stated there is no difference between a clitoral and vaginal orgasm and that all orgasms are the same physiologically. On the other hand, individual accounts sometimes reveal a more varied experience. What I hope becomes clearer to you, as you read this book, is that the structure of our genitals both inside and out is interconnected. As sex therapist Martha Kauppi puts it, physiologically, sexual arousal is simply a result of nerve stimulation and/or clitoral stimulation. And don't forget the huge power of what we do in our minds that can give a psychological and emotional boost to the whole experience.

Therefore my aim is not to convince you that these different types of orgasms exist or don't exist. Instead I hope to highlight some of the many types that women say they have experienced or that have been documented in studies. I also hope to give you a fuller picture of how nuanced orgasms can be.

I want you to keep in mind though that at the end of the day an orgasm is still an orgasm. This isn't the Olympics and you don't have to attempt or even think you 'should' aim to experience each of the different types that are said to be possible. The most useful approach is to increase knowledge and awareness with a playful and curious attitude towards your own experimentation.

Because there are numerous paths to orgasm and experiences of orgasms themselves, you can relax knowing that there is no 'right' way. As you will see, there are many ways. If you have experienced one type of orgasm, you might like to add in some other kind of stimulation to simply widen your experience and create more pleasure. Remember, this is what to focus on: Creating pleasure.

One of the possible reasons why women don't have a variety of orgasm experiences is because they are stuck in a monotonous routine with little variation or experimentation. Ancient texts on sexuality such as the Kama Sutra, urged people to explore and try out many different positions and experiences and the same still holds true today so you don't get stuck in a rut.

One of the mistakes a partner can make when touching a female sexually is to alter their touch at the moment when the female is getting really aroused. They might alter speed, pressure or location of touch. Doing this typically results in the built tension and arousal being lost. Don't make this mistake yourself when masturbating if you want to have an orgasm, especially if you are new to orgasms and still learning how your body responds. If something feels great and you can feel the pressure building then just keep doing it. It really can be that simple.

Clitoral

This is the type of orgasm that women are most often able to experience. 70% of women report that they require direct clitoral stimulation to orgasm and by that, they are generally referring to stimulation of the clitoral head. It has been suggested that women who have yet to experience an orgasm have simply not had their clitoris stimulated enough or at all during sex. On the one hand, this can mean the woman or partner is not directly or indirectly stimulating the clitoral head. And on the other hand, it can also imply that penetration is taking place before the woman is sufficiently aroused and before the full clitoris is engorged. Stimulating the internal legs and bulbs make penetration more pleasurable.

Time to play:

Getting to know your clitoris

Start by locating your clitoral head. If this is your first time, then either get out a mirror and find the little bud at the top of your labia, or find it by touch. Depending on your vulva, you may or may not have to separate the inner labia and lift the hood to reveal clitoral head.

Notice what it feels like to simply touch and press down on the head with your fingertip. Unless you're aroused, this is its neutral state when it isn't engorged. If your touch feels rough, add some lubricant to your finger and lighten your caresses. Remember this small bud is what is generally being referred to when someone talks or writes about the clitoris or clit.

Stroke down along each side and along the top of the hood, which covers and protects the head.

Pressing down and feeling from side to side above the head, can you feel the harder tissue underneath the hood? This is the clitoral shaft. Stimulating the shaft during masturbation can be arousing when direct clitoral contact feels too intense or when you just want to widen the range of sensations.

At the top of the shaft, the clitoris spreads out on each side with its legs. These follow alongside the pubic arch. The inner set of clitoral bulbs begin where the shaft and legs meet and lie along each side of the vaginal opening underneath the outer labia. Because of their internal location, you can indirectly stimulate the clitoral legs and bulbs by making a peace sign and stroking the entire length of the outer labia from the top of the clitoral head to the vaginal opening. When aroused, feel inside your vagina and press against each side. As you do this, you are also pressing up against the bulbs. As the bulbs become engorged, the vaginal opening can become narrower as each bulb 'hugs' the opening. When using a vibrator or dildo that fills you completely, any movement that rubs up or vibrates against each side is also stimulating the clitoral bulbs.

The clitoral head, shaft, legs and bulbs all contain erectile tissue, which becomes firm and erect when you are aroused. The legs and bulbs are covered in muscle tissue, which also contributes to the feeling of sexual tension and contracts when you orgasm.

The more you practice becoming familiar and in touch with the various parts of the clitoris and sensations of stimulating it externally as well as internally, the more you are heightening your capacity for sexual pleasure.

Vaginal

For most women, the vaginal orgasm is an elusive one. While many pleasurable sensations can be had from penetration, for most women penetration is not enough to create an orgasm by itself. Thinking you should be able to have an orgasm from penetrative sex alone can lead to unnecessary feelings of inadequacy and frustration.

With one in three children accessing online pornography by the age of 10, it has become common for teenagers and young adults to have little understanding of what 'real life' sexual experiences are like or could be like unless they have had access to proper sex education. And for those of us born before online pornography, we've had the same incorrect 'teaching' through the sex scenes on TV and in the movies. The majority of sex scenes in both show women having incredible orgasms through just a short amount of thrusting.

In the Hite report (a study of female sexual experiences), only 29% of women reported being able to orgasm through intercourse alone. The basic missionary position doesn't create the right amount of stimulation for most women unless they are already very aroused and their clitoris (external and internal) are stimulated in some way. Interestingly, research using 3-D sonography revealed that due to the clitoris's extensive size internally, when a woman experiences a vaginal orgasm, she is most likely actually having a clitoral orgasm, because the internal parts of the clitoris are being stimulated.

The vaginal orgasm is reached by stimulation of the interior walls of the vagina including the paraurethral tissue (G-spot) and hypogastric nerve plexus. Women who have reached their mid-thirties tend to experience orgasms during vaginal penetration more often than those in their twenties. It is debated whether this is the result of hormonal changes, which occur in the early thirties, or if it has more to do with women generally becoming less anxious about sex and their bodies with age and getting better at knowing and asking for what they want in bed. And what we don't know is how many of those women are stimulating the clitoral head at the same time as the penetration!

Time to play:

Igniting vaginal sensations

As you masturbate and become aroused, place a vibrator or dildo inside your vagina. It should be wide enough that you feel it rest comfortably against your internal 'walls'. Stop any other stimulation and with the toy resting inside you, bring your attention to the sensations you feel inside. Using only small hip movements and pelvic floor muscle contractions see if you can feel the toy against your G-spot, against each side wall and along the lower wall towards your buttocks. Once you have tuned in to these sensations, increase stimulation by adding vibration.

Don't expect to suddenly experience a vaginal orgasm if you've never had one before. Accept that you may or may not (ever) experience an orgasm through vaginal stimulation alone. However, what is within your power is the ability to increase your focus and thus awareness of vaginal sensations through practice. In addition, the more you stimulate yourself vaginally, the more pleasurable nerve endings you will activate inside. This will also increase general enjoyment with vaginal stimulation.

Coital alignment technique (CAT)

One way to increase the amount of clitoral stimulation during intercourse is by changing the position. A classic example of a clitoral stimulating position is the coital alignment technique (CAT). The CAT position is an adaptation of the missionary position, which creates more pressure and rubbing against the area from the pubic bone down to the vaginal opening.

The penetrating person lies on top with legs in between their partner below as in missionary. The person on top then shifts forward a few inches so that the base of the penis or strap-on is in contact with the clitoral head and shaft. The pelvis of the person underneath is tilted upwards through this shift, which makes wrapping legs around her partner's body an option or her legs can be straight or bent. Together in this position you're aiming for a grinding and rocking motion rather than thrusting.

You can explore the CAT during masturbation with any toy that allows for simultaneous penetration and rubbing against the clitoral head.

G-spot (Paraurethral tissue)

This is the sensitive zone a few inches inside the vagina towards the front of your body. If you find it hard to reach with your own fingers, a partner or vibrator can stimulate it for you. Explore what feels good for you, especially when you are already aroused. When this area is stimulated, some women experience a feeling similar to needing to urinate. It is usually through G-spot stimulation that some women ejaculate upon orgasm. You can refer back to the section entitled 'Anatomy of Arousal' if you want to revise and learn more about the paraurethral tissue.

71

Time to play:

<u>Locating your G-spot</u>

Lying on your back, insert your index or middle finger deeply inside your vagina. Use lubrication to ease insertion.

With the palm of your hand facing up, curl the inserted finger to touch against the front wall of your vagina. Caress this front vaginal wall from vaginal entrance to deeper in while seeking an area of tissue that feels spongy and rougher in texture compared to that around it. Depending on your personal anatomy, this may be easy or hard to reach with your finger.

Take note of the difference in sensation as you mimic penetration by gliding a finger or vibrator in and out and brush against this area, compared to deliberately pressing up against it. To directly stimulate it further, play around with making a 'come here' beckoning motion with your finger and exploring movements like rubbing in circles, pressing, and tapping against it. You might like to use a curved G-spot vibrator or a regular vibrator held at an angle, so that the tip is held against this sensitive spot.

A-spot

Remember, this is an area inside the vagina further up from the G-spot, and nearer to the cervix, which can also be a source of pleasure due to the stimulation of the hypogastric nerve plexus. Beyond its role in enhancing pleasure, A-spot researcher Dr. Chua Chee Ann was interested specifically in this area's usefulness in increasing vaginal lubrication for anyone experiencing vaginal dryness, whether young or old. Controversially, he suggests daily massage of the A-spot as a technique to promote arousal despite the woman's emotional state or relationship happiness. In contrast, I strongly encourage you during solo play and sexual exploration with a partner to listen to your thoughts and emotions, approach sexuality with love and gentleness and always listen to what does and doesn't feel right for you at any given moment.

Time to play:

Explore your A-spot

After locating your G-spot, reach further into the vagina along the front wall. Locate your cervix deep inside your vagina (the lower part of the uterus that extends into the vagina). The cervix feels firm and has a tubular or circular shape.

Press against your vagina's front wall just beyond the start of the cervix. Dr. Chua advises a gentle stroking and application of pressure to this deep frontal wall until you begin to lubricate. Then, with an in-and-out movement, rub gently along the front wall from the A-spot back down to the G-spot and back up. Dr. Chua suggests daily stimulation for 5-10 minutes for increased lubrication and arousal.

Other 'types' of orgasms

Multiple

Many women are capable of learning to become multi-orgasmic if they choose to put the time and energy into it. For some women, multiple orgasms are experienced back-to-back as a kind of rolling, longer orgasm and for others, there can be a pause in between each orgasm. In contrast to men, women can have multiple orgasms, because the female body doesn't experience a refractory period. In men, this refractory period hinders their ability to have consecutive orgasms after ejaculation. However, men can learn to have multiple orgasms by learning how to separate their orgasm from ejaculation, which happens around 3 seconds after orgasm. It's the ejaculation that causes their refractory period. But let's get back to the female body.

Whether you do or don't experience multiple orgasms can depend on whether you continue stimulation while having an orgasm or after a short pause in order to continue your sexual arousal. Continuing stimulation can cause arousal to build up quickly to the next orgasm. Some women haven't experienced multiple orgasms, because they stop touching themselves upon orgasm or, if they rely on their partner for stimulation, it may be their partner who stops the touch.

Over time, as you continue to work on your sexual exploration, become more and more in touch with your own body's responses. Get to know your preferred touch, your personal arousal signals, and gain more body and genital acceptance. Multiple orgasms can become a reality with any sexual practice, not only through following the exercise below.

As with all of this book's exercises, I urge you to approach exploration of multiple orgasms with an attitude of curiosity, patience, acceptance of where ever you are on your sexual exploration journey, and loving dedication to pleasure. Learning to have multiple orgasms can take time, so you might as well make sure you're enjoying every step along the way and see it as just one part of the bigger picture. This is about you claiming your sexuality and sexual expression as a natural part of who you are as a person.

Time to play:

<u>Riding the wave</u>

The next time you are masturbating and about to orgasm, become very mindful of the movements you are making with your hands and any toys as well as your body, such as clenching or rocking. Consciously tune in to the sensations as you feel the orgasm roll through you. Instead of stopping touch, continue the same movements while you orgasm.

You may feel a slight 'coming down' from the first orgasm while you keep up the stimulation before the arousal rises again or you might have a second (and third) orgasm directly following the first. Either is possible and okay. The key is, if the stimulation still feels good, keep it up and if you notice you need or want something different, then add in different movements or stimulation until you feel the subsequent orgasm rolling in after the first. Some women say they can reach subsequent orgasms using the same stimulation they used for the first one, whereas others say, they have to treat each orgasm (and the build-up to each) as completely different experiences. In the latter case, that means they have to use different techniques in order to reach each orgasm.

If you find that continuing the same movement during the point of orgasm is too intense or creates discomfort in any way, either decrease pressure, speed and location of touch or move from direct to more indirect stimulation. For example, let's say you orgasm first by rubbing your clitoris (the head) in an up and down motion, which then becomes too intense. You could swap to a circular movement around the clitoris or pulse gently with your fingers either side of it. You could make soft strokes along your clitoral hood, continue (or start) insertion of a finger or vibrator into the vagina, or gently squeeze and release your vaginal muscles. Try any of the above swaps as well as any other ideas mentioned elsewhere in the book. The idea is to continue stimulation in whichever way you can to keep arousal high.

Short pause

Another way of experiencing multiple orgasms can be created by having a short break after an orgasm. This break might last anything from a few seconds to several minutes. During this break, you fully give in to the climax of the orgasm and part of the come-down (resolution phase). Then after enjoying this short break, you restart stimulation.

Try this out by enjoying the orgasm rolling through your body and the subsequent sense of calm and relaxation as your muscles continue to quiver and spasm less and less with every breath. And before they die down completely, resume stimulation.

As in the above 'riding the wave' exercise, you might be able to start up with the exact same movements as before or you may have to make adjustments according to sensitivity or responsiveness to touch.

Nocturnal

Similar to wet dreams, vaginal lubrication is a normal occurrence during the stage of sleep, which includes dreaming (REM sleep). Although there is no way to consciously experience a nocturnal orgasm unless you are a skilled lucid dreamer or lucky enough to wake up at the right moment, some women have been found to orgasm in their sleep.

While we can't necessarily dictate to our subconscious what we want to dream at night, our dream content often contains themes and emotions connected to our current experiences. As you explore and expand your sexual experiences in masturbation and in fantasies, there is a chance that your subconscious will be processing it at some point as you sleep.

Therefore if you want to have more sexy dreams and increase the chance that you join the nocturnal orgasm's club there are various ways to go about this. None of this is scientifically proven by the way.

Time to play:

<u>Encouraging nocturnal orgasms and dreams</u>

Firstly, give sex and your sexual experience space to be expressed during the day; most if not every day. Using techniques and ideas from this book, do at least one thing every day to connect in with your sexuality. This may be as simple as sensually caressing yourself while soaping up in the shower, daydreaming with sexual fantasies or tuning into the sensations of your skin against clothing or air on your erogenous zones.

Secondly, give your sexual exploration and growth meaning and importance. Connect emotionally with the reasons why your sexual expression and development is important to you. If you haven't thought about this in depth before, take some quiet time now to think it through and write down your answers.

Notice what emotions and motivations come up as you ask yourself the following:

– What prompted me to buy this book?
– What was I taught about sex, orgasms and sexual expression while growing up?
– Why is this important to me as an individual… and as a woman?
– What personal experiences from my past have highlighted the importance of claiming my sexuality for

myself?

– What will growing my comfort with and confidence in my sexuality enable in other areas of my life? – What much bigger goal is my sexual growth part of?

– What are my sexual goals?

– What new sexual experience would I like to have?

Formulate a strong emotional connection with why your sexuality is important to you personally and remember this each time you masturbate, read this book or do any of the exercises. The emotional boost and drive towards your sexual growth will create richer pathways in the brain and boost the likelihood of nighttime processing.

And remember to read erotic stories. Have you ever watched a horror movie just before bed and had nightmares with a similar theme? In the same way, if you watch erotic films or read erotica before bed the theme or elements of the story line might follow you into your dreams.

Fantasy

A very small percentage (around 2%) of women report being able to orgasm without any touch but through fantasizing and thoughts alone. Even if it's not enough to give you an orgasm, for the other 98% fantasy can nonetheless play an important role in boosting arousal as well as developing and maintaining a connection with one's sexuality.

We will explore using fantasy as an arousal enhancement technique later in this book.

Faked

Pretending you've had an orgasm when you haven't can be much more complicated than it seems at face value. Individual reasons are varied and include wanting to give your lover an ego-boost, copying what you've seen in porn, because you think that's how you 'should' sound or act, wanting to avoid the topic of your own pleasure, because you don't know what works for you, or simply hoping to speed up the process, because you're bored, uncomfortable or in pain. Lili Loofbourow highlighted another perspective in her article *The Female Price of Male Pleasure* published in The Week. She stated that women feeling the need to fake orgasms is part of a much larger societal issue. It's just the tip of the iceberg of female and male relationships and the power play that can exist in them.

Regardless of the reason behind faking it, one of the problems that arises from doing so is that your sexual partner thinks they have learned what it takes to create what appears to be a wonderful experience for you and are likely to continue touching you in that same way in the future. It can become hard to stop faking with someone once you've started, and more of a challenge to ask for what you want.

If you have the courage to step outside of your comfort zone, you're likely to discover how much more empowering it is to be honest with someone about what is really going on for you during sex. You're giving you and your partner the chance to address any underlying concerns, to explore and adapt the way you've been having sex and you can also start practicing the important skill of being able to ask for what you want during sex. If you have been faking orgasms, I encourage you to find a way to have the option to enjoy sex without an orgasm and without faking one.

Time to play:

<u>Exploring your reasons for faking it</u>

Get a pen and paper. Think back over your relationships and sexual encounters when you have faked an orgasm. Write down a list of the reasons you faked it. It might take some time to reflect and remember. Be honest with yourself and allow all answers that come to mind.

<u>What works?</u>

If you have also had experiences where you have had orgasms, then also write down the key elements in those situations. You might find yourself writing things like "I trusted them", "I felt comfortable", "There wasn't any pressure", "It was loving and caring", "We used lots of lube", "We were just playing". Or you might have completely different reasons. Just be curious and notice what was important to you during the sexual experiences that put you at ease, where you felt comfortable to communicate your needs and confident to focus on pleasure. Notice the details of what allowed you to have an orgasm.

<u>What might work?</u>

If you have only ever faked orgasms, then ask yourself what you would need in order to be able to feel okay to say things like: "I'm okay if I don't have an orgasm", "Can I give you a hand with that?", "Can we try a different position", "Can we slow down", "I'm not really into this", "Can you do that softer/more to the left/higher/lower". What other sentences would you like to be able to say during sex? And what do you imagine would allow you to be honest about your orgasm experience or lack thereof? What would you need in the situation and what would you need from your partner?

With your insights from the past, focus on the elements that are important to you during sex and identify how you can create the right setting for yourself. Revisit the section on accelerators and brakes. What did you learn about yourself there? Part of getting what you want might entail having a conversation with your partner about how to make sex more enjoyable. It will likely be extremely helpful to share your ideas of what would make you more relaxed and comfortable, and able to take your foot off the brake so you can put your foot on the accelerator and get turned on. You might also come to the conclusion that you need to do some healing work on old memories for example by seeing a sex or couples therapist together or by yourself. You could discuss ways in which you can transform your sex life and let go of old habits that no longer serve you.

Orgasms according to sensation – another way to think about it

In addition to orgasm types labeled according to how they are triggered, orgasms can also be described according to their characteristics. Here are some examples of this category:

Peak orgasms

Reached through the addition of the tensing of muscles and sometimes holding the breath just before and during an orgasm. This can create a more intense physiological response.

Relaxation orgasms

The type of orgasm that is experienced during spiritual or mindfulness practices that focus on elements such as energy flow, breath and connection. A relaxation orgasm can also happen on a lazy weekend morning when no-one is rushing to go anywhere.

Older couples sometimes discover this kind of relaxed climax later in life through the sheer need to slow down due to their bodies requiring more time to become fully aroused. There can be a spiritual awakening as they discover this laid-back, slow lovemaking where they relax fully into it and take all the time they need. Other times, people experience relaxation orgasms when their children move out of home and they realize they have the house to themselves and can luxuriate in sexual pleasure.

Pressure orgasms

As the name implies, this is an orgasm which follows an element of pressure such as squeezing the thighs together, rocking or indirect stimulation of some kind.

So, after reading about all of these different types of orgasms. What are your thoughts now? My hope is that it helps you realize there are multiple paths to climaxing and that through play and experimentation you can discover what feels good for you. Whether touch leads to an orgasm or not isn't as important as embracing your sexual arousal.

I'm going to say it again: Being able to experience any type of orgasm is great. Enjoy whatever 'type' you may have or even just let go of the aim of reaching an orgasm altogether. Focus your attention on creating pleasure-filled sensations and a nurturing approach to your sexual pleasure.

Remember, you don't actually need to orgasm to have a completely enjoyable sex life. In fact, many women who know how to reach orgasm choose to forgo it sometimes when making love. It is only one aspect of all the potential experiences possible during intimate touch.

7. Don't only focus on the goal – enjoy the journey!

Regardless of the reasons why you masturbate, one of the most useful approaches to take is to enjoy each moment as you experience it. For example, some women masturbate specifically to give themselves an orgasm or to learn how to have one. This is absolutely fine. At the same time, it can become problematic if you start to focus on or stress about how long you are taking, expect certain results or if you think in terms of whether you are 'succeeding' or not.

Stressful thinking doesn't help. An almost guaranteed way to lose arousal during the build-up phase to orgasm is feeling stress and anxiety. This is why it is useful to practice and learn to slow down and be mentally and physically in the moment, because otherwise you might sabotage the chance to have an orgasm in the first place. Due to stressful thinking you might also miss out on enjoying some of the experience. Women who become focused on reaching goals when masturbating, can also encounter similar problems during intimacy with a partner. Rather than just enjoying it as an experience of pleasuring each other and connecting intimately, they may think they need to help their partner orgasm as quickly as possible and may fake an orgasm themselves in order to hurry things along.

People can get so focused on sexual goals that they miss opportunities for fun, new experiences and emotional connection. Even orgasmic couples who aren't experiencing any current problems in their sex life can become unsatisfied if sex becomes monotonous or too focused on the goal of each having an orgasm. By masturbating with the aim of simply experiencing pleasure and connection with your sexual self, you will enjoy an increase in overall pleasure and funnily enough are more likely to discover blissful sensations and reach orgasm easier, because you have removed the pressure. That doesn't mean you shouldn't aim to have an orgasm when having sex or masturbating – in fact aiming for an orgasm has shown in studies to increase your likelihood of having one – just hold back from making it the *only* goal.

Here's the thing: It's like kids on a road trip. You could be passing through an incredible, breathtakingly gorgeous landscape and the kids keep asking "Are we there yet?" In this example, the kids are neither noticing nor appreciating the ever changing view, enjoying the feeling of resting back with their head against the seat, or focusing on whatever conversations are taking place at that moment in time. They are focused on the future instead and whatever it is that they want to do once they arrive. They miss out on so much, because they're unable to tap into the pleasure that can be had from the journey. In fact, their constant noticing of the time it's taking to get there can turn the whole driving experience into a negative one!

As kids grow into adults, many learn to slow down and appreciate the journey and as a result their holiday experience can begin the moment they leave home. It's exactly the same with masturbation and sexual pleasure. Don't dismiss the start nor the middle parts as boring or unimportant through over-focusing on any desired results. Focus in on the whole experience and enjoy the ride!

Time to play:

Timed pleasure

Set a timer for 10 minutes. Masturbate for this time with the sole intention of relaxing and focusing on your bodily sensations. This is not about trying to make yourself orgasm but for you to strengthen your mental ability to tune into yourself, stay with your touch, the sensations and increase calm, focused awareness.

There is no correct way to touch yourself when doing this exercise and it is completely normal for your mind to wander. When it does, gently bring your attention back to your body, your breath and the sensations you are feeling.

Explore the senses: Feel the touch of your body against the skin of your fingertips and the presence of your fingers against your vulva. What can you hear? Not just in the environment around you, but can you also hear your breathing or other sounds from within? Is the movement of touch creating any sounds itself? And if you enjoy visualizing, you could also imagine in your mind's eye what the movements look like.

After the time is up, take a moment to check in with yourself and what you discovered. It might be an affirmation of a type of touch you enjoy or you may have surprised yourself by realizing something for the first time.

If you feel that you could benefit from more of this kind of focusing on sensations, then try out the exercises later in the book called Sensate Focus exercises.

Specific focus

Set a timer for five minutes and in this time, all you are going to do is touch one part of your body with continued focus.

Choose the area of your body that you are going to focus on today. It could be just one side of your labia, an inner thigh, the sole of your foot, palm of your hand, your forehead or lips. I encourage you to repeat this exercise with different parts of the body to really explore it.

Do not move to other parts of your body within the five minutes, even if you want to! This is an important exercise for learning how to focus on body sensations and find pleasure in micro movements. It's also helpful as a body-based meditation for women whose minds drift during sex.

As you touch yourself, use different amounts of pressure from pressing down to feather-light strokes and vary the contact point of your fingers. Use your fingertips as well as the flat pads of your fingers. Also explore the sensation of resting your palm on the area and feeling the warm contact without movement.

Any time your mind wanders, bring it back to the touch and the pleasurable sensations you are experiencing.

Check how you feel before and after doing this exercise – mentally, emotionally and physically.

Partner variation 1:

Masturbate as described above but this time with a partner watching. Set the scene in a way that will make it comfortable for you both. This may include dimming lights, putting on some relaxing music, lying next to each other, and ensuring you won't be disturbed by phone alerts. Create a setting that will work for you.

In this variation, you will each take five minutes, one after the other to touch yourselves (not each other) in a way that is only about exploration, pleasure and maintaining focus on your own body and its responses. Remember, there is no expectation to climax while doing this and it is useful to agree not to moan or do anything you might do only to please your partner – only naturally occurring sounds are allowed. When it is your turn to masturbate, you can choose to have your eyes open or closed.

The role of the non-masturbating partner in this exercise is to simply observe how your partner is using touch to pleasure themselves.

As you take the role of the observer, I encourage you to follow your partner's breath and breathe in time with them to increase a sense of connection.

Remember, the masturbating person's role is simply to touch and explore in a pleasurable way. Share your experiences with each other once you have each taken a turn touching yourself. Let each other know what you learned. Discuss how easy or challenging it was to watch or be watched. What feelings came up when it was your turn to masturbate? How can you use this experience to enhance sex together?

Partner variation 2:

Take turns masturbating each other for 10 minutes. The focus in this exercise is on giving (when you are the giver) and receiving (when you are the receiver).

Set clear boundaries in advance. This is an exercise about enjoying pleasure without feeling obligated to pleasure your partner at the same time as being pleasured yourself. Doing this means that you can be 100% focused on yourself as you are being touched.

Remember this is an exploratory exercise, so avoid any unnecessary talking during the 10 minutes unless your partner is doing something you really don't like. If that is the case, then keep any feedback to one or two sentences such as "Hmm, my clit is a bit too sensitive, can you touch my labia instead?", or "Softer please". Understand from the start that the person being touched is allowed to simply lie there and enjoy touch without talking.

Note: When doing these partner exercises you may want to take a moment after each of you have had your turn, in order to give positive feedback. This can include what you liked seeing, what touch you found most enjoyable and how you felt sharing this experience together.

8. Masturbation through the lifetime

Childhood

Do you know the children's song "Heads, shoulders, knees and toes, knees and toes"? Well, when it comes to body exploration and kids it's often more like "Heads, nostrils, ears, mouths, shoulders, stomachs, penises/vulvas, knees and toes, knees and toes". Regardless of their sex or gender, from a very young age children will be exploring their bodies with curiosity, which includes their genitals. Babies in utero have even been observed touching their genitals. All this body touching is part of learning about ourselves and familiarizing ourselves with what feels good and how things work – from day one .

As we get older, self-touch becomes more purposeful. When a child explores their body, they're trying to work out not only how it works but also in which ways it's the same as or different from others. It's common and normal to play games of 'I'll show you mine if you show me yours' with other kids and to be wanting to repeat actions that feel good, such as noticing that rubbing their hips against something feels nice.

When growing up, if you had caregivers comfortable with the topic of sex and bodies, you would have had supportive comments when found touching yourself and conversations that felt so normal you might not even remember them. How our parents respond to our curiosity can shape our beliefs and feelings about sex well into our adult years. Unfortunately, many of us get the message either directly or indirectly that touching ourselves is bad, naughty, dangerous, shameful or wrong in some way. When this happens, we are more likely to struggle with being completely relaxed about our sexuality as an adult. Ideally, we'd all grow up learning the correct names of our genitals, understand about health and hygiene and know that bodies are different and unique. We'd also be taught that some parts of our body are private, that it's normal to feel good about our bodies and that we can gain a lot of pleasure from them too.

As already mentioned, the current reality is that the average age of seeing porn for the first time is 10 years old. While some adults seek to protect their children from sex altogether and keep them unaware of sexuality, the problem is that children are inquisitive and will just get their information and sex education elsewhere. That source often ends up being the playground, because children are wondering and talking together about bodies and sex from an early age, regardless of conversations with their parents. If a parent chooses to overcome their own discomfort and talk to their child about sex, they can then ensure their child is getting correct and age-appropriate information to help them understand this important and complex topic. It also means that if they are told or shown something disturbing about sex by someone else, the child is more likely to reach out to their parent and ask for clarification about what they've heard or seen.

The role that self-touch and early sexual exploration plays is far-reaching in our childhood. We're laying the foundation for knowing our bodies, our responses, what we like and what our early fantasies are. It's also a time of discovering what our sexual orientation is. All of this self-discovery helps us as we come into the adolescent phase of our lives.

Teenage years

Do you remember your first masturbation experiences? For some they took place in their childhood and for others not until they were teenagers (and for some, not even then). Teenage years are when early explorations typically get expanded and fine-tuned. Masturbation is the main type of sexual activity for a teenager and yet, from a developmental viewpoint, it plays the role of rehearsal for partner sex. As a teenager works out more and more how their body works and what feels good, they are gaining knowledge that they can eventually teach to a sexual partner. Teenagers are naturally interested in becoming skilled in and satisfied from sexual experiences and their continued 'research' in self-pleasure supports this goal. Look at teen magazines and you'll see this interest fed through articles on sex, sexuality, sex terms and stories of readers' experiences.

As a female teenager uses self-pleasure to satisfy their developing sexual desire, they're also solidifying their first techniques and the situations that they fantasize about. They're learning how to reach orgasm through masturbation and their preferences such as direct or indirect touch to the clitoris. At some point during these years, most people start putting what they've learned by themselves into practice with someone else.

When this stage of further discovery and growing development in one's sexuality is skipped for any reason, people may report challenges in their adult sex life including the inability to orgasm. It makes sense; how can we know ourselves sexually if we have never explored our bodies with touch, fantasized or talked about sex growing up? As each of us is so different, it is risky to assume that someone else (of any sex) will know the fine details of what turns us on personally. This is one of the reasons why getting to know ourselves in a sexual way can be so beneficial.

Adult years

Masturbation in our adult years can continue to develop as a source of self-exploration and discovery. What we find sexy as a teenager might be similar or different to what we discover about our fantasies as adults. With growing maturity and changing lives, self-pleasure can also be a source of self-care no matter the relationship status.

Masturbation is good for us emotionally, physically and mentally. With increasing work hours and expectations, masturbation with orgasm releases tension and stress, helps against insomnia and depression and can also be used as a way to lessen period-related discomfort. If you're in a relationship and you have a higher libido than your partner, it's also an easy way to meet your sexual needs. Masturbation in adult years can be a handy option if your partner is tired, ill or not in the mood for sexual intimacy.

If you need some kind of medical endorsement, know that having regular intimacy with yourself or others brings blood flow to your pelvis, helps keep the tissues strong and thick and your pelvic floor muscles strong as well as flexible. Masturbation and orgasms exercise your circulatory system and nervous system and promote good health. It's so good for us that sex experts Ellen Barnard and Myrtle Wilhite (sexualityresources.com) recommend a weekly orgasm for overall well-being.

Some women are discovering masturbation, sensuality and sexual celebration as a path to embracing their femininity and sexuality in adulthood. It can be a game changer to view masturbation as a method that you use to soothe and care for yourself as well as boost your body acceptance. You can start doing this by setting a clear intention of using masturbation as an act of self-love.

During and post pregnancy

Pregnancy – With its hormonal changes, pregnancy can be a time when some women (but definitely not all) experience heightened libido. It's also a time when masturbation is still completely normal and natural. Self-pleasure during pregnancy can be a wonderful way to relax and enjoy pleasurable sensations whether by yourself or as part of partner sex.

There are a couple of things that are important to pay attention to when masturbating during pregnancy, namely cleanliness and timeliness. It's important to ensure that any objects you insert into your vagina are clean and washed with soapy water or covered with a fresh condom to make sure you're not upsetting the bacteria-yeast balance of the vagina. Nails should also be clean, trimmed and/or smooth to minimize the chance of infections. In terms of timeliness, it is important to discuss the safety of orgasms with your health professional during the late stages of pregnancy. In moderate or high-risk pregnancies with, for example, a risk of pre-term labor or difficulty controlling blood pressure, it's likely you will be advised to refrain from orgasms.

Perineal massage by hand can be part of an effective preparation for vaginal birth and could be something you integrate as part of your self-pleasuring sessions. Massaging this area with a water-based lube can promote flexibility and durability of the skin and underlying muscles and will help the vaginal opening stretch as your baby enters the world. Talk to your healthcare professional to get a specific plan for how to do this in a way that is best for you.

After pregnancy – This is a time when women often report having zero time for themselves and it feels like someone always wants something from them. They might say their body doesn't feel like it belongs to them anymore.

The time after giving birth it is understandably a period when sexual pleasure isn't high on the priority list. Regardless of the birth process, the body is still healing and it can be harmful to engage in some sexual acts early on. Therefore, monitor your body's recovery with your healthcare professional and ask them for specifics in relation to your body's healing and what is safe to do.

Although penetration is generally the last sexual act to come back into play post birth, masturbation is one of the safest ways to reconnect with your sexual self. Masturbation also allows you to gently observe and notice your readiness for sexual intimacy with someone else. The free Vaginal Renewal ® Program, originally designed for menopausal women, can also be used for keeping the skin around scarring stretchy and elastic as part of episiotomy recovery (when the perineum has been cut to facilitate childbirth). Once again, if in doubt ask your health professional, especially if you're noticing something has changed in your body's arousal process or if anything hurts during sex. Ellen and Myrtle at A Woman's Touch are also a wonderful source of free advice and information and will gladly help if you get in touch with them. If you're in a relationship, the postpartum period can also a good time to get support from a couples counselor as you navigate your new roles as parents and the changes to your sex life.

During and post menopause

Another big hormonal event for women is menopause (whether surgically induced or natural). The change in hormones (both estrogen and testosterone) has a direct effect on our genital health, which can create havoc in a woman's sex life and her experience of herself as a sexual being. If left misunderstood, unchecked and untreated, some women give up on their sex life altogether. Menopausal changes can lead to issues involving genital pain from dryness and atrophy (thinning) of the vaginal skin, painful penetration, a dramatically lowered sensation of orgasm, reduced libido and pelvic floor muscles that become either tight or weak.

The timing of natural menopause also often coincides with an emotional time in a woman's life where she might still be supporting her children as well as having elderly parents requiring increasing support. Having teenagers in the house can also highlight the confronting reality of the end of one's own fertility.

In order to hold on to her sexual health and vitality through menopause, a woman has to accept the natural changes that take place in her body rather than ignore them. Through acceptance, she is then able to work with the changes and support her body during this time. Masturbation can serve as a great tool to track individual changes as well as continue to be a source of pleasure and a way to help keep the vaginal tissues healthy.

So what can be done to hold on to sexuality during this time? Firstly, adopting a mindset of curiosity and acceptance will go a long way. Know that change is going to happen and be curious about the ways you notice the changes. The more you notice, the more you can then explain to a healthcare professional (such as a pelvic floor physiotherapist) to ensure they can give you the help you might need.

Secondly, be patient with yourself during masturbation and sex. This is a time when many women find they start needing longer and increased stimulation before the vagina becomes lubricated enough for penetration. You can boost sexual pleasure and improve the sensations of touch by adding some lubrication as well. Water-based lubes are great for adding moisture, and silicone-based lubes help lock that moisture in. You can use them separately as well as experiment with a hybrid product that is both water-based and contains silicone. The goal is to create slipperiness inside and out to reduce friction for penetration (whether a finger, toy or penis) as well as allow silky smooth touch on the labia and clitoris. Isn't it funny to think how so many menopausal women automatically moisturize their faces and hands on a daily basis to stop the skin from drying out and to help their skin look and feel plumped but don't realize that the vaginal skin needs the same!

Thirdly, because the sexual response is slowing down during this time in our lives, make sure to remember that the power of a vibrator can cut the time to orgasm in half. While it's not a race, a vibrator can play a huge role in keeping masturbation an easy source of joy and relaxation. Did you know that vibration against the skin also helps strengthen it to withstand sideways pressure (such as experienced during any penetration or rubbing). This quality in skin is called 'shear strength'. Shear strength in skin including inside the vagina can reduce during menopause as estrogen levels drop. When estrogen levels drop and shear strength of the skin is weakened as a result, some women experience tearing of the vaginal skin during intimacy. This can be prevented and even rehabilitated by regular use of a vibrator (with a low vibration) inside the vagina, because it literally improves the shear strength of the vaginal tissue. Even if penetrative sex or masturbation isn't your thing, the difference between having healthy vaginal tissue or not may also be felt during medical examinations and in general daily life as the skin rubs against itself as we walk, move and get up and down from a seat.

And finally, remember that sexual functioning and arousal are cardiovascular events. You can directly boost your blood flow by taking a 15 minute walk before sexual play. This has shown to increase sexual satisfaction by a whopping 38%! Testosterone also plays a role in the body's ability to feel sexual sensations, which is a great motivator for taking up resistance training (lifting weights to build muscle), because this increases the testosterone you produce. In addition, if you aren't already eating a predominantly plant-based diet, you can improve your sexual health through eating a low-inflammation diet such as the Mediterranean diet with an abundance of fruit, vegetables, whole grains, legumes, nuts and seeds and only low – if any – amounts of animal products.

If you're wondering how to put all of this into action in a practical, therapeutic way, check out the Vaginal Renewal ® Program at A Woman's Touch. Their unique self-administered program is a hormone-free, non-pharmaceutical and free to access program that only requires a vibrator with a low speed 'throbby' vibration (proven to rehabilitate skin), lubricants and your time. I've mentioned this program a lot in this book, because it is in invaluable tool that has helped many women around the world – often in cases when women don't even know there is something they can do to relieve their symptoms.

Elderly years

Embodying sexuality in its many forms into our final years is very much a matter of having decided it is something you want and are willing to work for. How you've treated your body up to now will be having a big effect and showing in your experience as an older person – in your range of movement and health of mind and body.

Hopefully as your body has aged, you have learned how to keep your genitals supple and healthy with programs such as the Vaginal Renewal ® Program, as well as connecting with health experts such as pelvic floor physiotherapists to support healthy muscular functioning of the pelvic floor. However, due to embarrassment or lack of information, some women ignore the changes or think that they're too old to deserve sexual satisfaction.

In this case, there is a challenge ahead but reclaiming sexuality is not impossible. You just need to let go of your old perceptions of what sex and masturbation 'should' be like and realize that your ability for sexual pleasure hasn't disappeared – it's just different and you will need to give it some loving attention.

Patience will be your best friend as will owning and using a vibrator as you age. In your elderly years an orgasm is likely to take longer than it did when you were younger, because of changes in your hormones and body functioning. An orgasm is, however, still possible so long as your body is healthy with good cardiovascular functioning (to get the blood flow into the genitals) and pelvic floor muscles still able to contract and release. Keep in mind that an inability to orgasm or get physically aroused can indicate an urgent medical matter to discuss with your doctor such as heart disease or diabetes or medication that might need to be adjusted.

As with any age, remember 70% of women require direct clitoral stimulation in order to reach orgasm, and using a vibrator reduces the time to orgasm in half. I know I keep pointing this out, but it's an important fact to remember. Other physical steps you can take to support having orgasms in your later years include exercising before any intimate play to help bring blood flow to your genitals and have regular dates with your vibrator. The more often your body becomes aroused and experiences an orgasm, the easier it becomes to continue having them. You could also experiment with avoiding eating before you masturbate or have sexual play, because eating directs the blood flow to your digestive system, rather than your genitals. In addition, looking after your emotional and mental health supports sexual health. Anxiety is a desire killer and if you put pressure on yourself in any way, getting aroused and having an orgasm becomes so much harder.

No matter your age or health status, you have the right

to be able to express yourself sexually. Feel entirely within your rights to request that a retirement or elderly-care facility provide you with privacy. In a practical sense, this might mean arranging with staff that they do not disturb you for a certain period of time on your request or make accommodations to allow you to have a partner share your bed.

As you age from childhood and adolescence, through your adult years and times of hormonal upheaval into your golden years, sexual exploration and expression remains a birthright. Just as the experience of dating and sex changes with age and maturity, so too does our solo expression of sexuality. I invite you to enjoy the ongoing journey of your maturing sexual self all the way into your future. Give yourself full permission to continue discovering your body's potential for pleasure. Learn and accept your body in its beautiful uniqueness and unearth masturbation as a way to connect with your sensuality. Give yourself permission to use masturbation as an expression of love and care towards yourself. With this gift to yourself, self-pleasure can become a place of pleasure you can return to again and again and again.

9. Working through psychological challenges

Psychological challenges can get in the way of us having carefree sexual exploration at any age. I recommend that you consider having sessions with a therapist to work through any personal challenges. You may also wish to start the healing process by learning about how various psychological concerns and challenges can affect sexual expression and discovering some steps you can take yourself.

History of abuse or trauma

Some people find creative ways to reclaim and empower themselves after traumatic experiences. Unfortunately that's not the case for everyone. Trauma can linger in our subconscious for years after the original experience/s in an attempt to protect and keep ourselves safe. Abuse can come in many forms: Sexual, emotional, spiritual, psychological and physical. These forms can on their own and in combination have an effect on how we see ourselves as sexual beings as well as how comfortable we are with intimacy, even being intimate with ourselves.

Abuse and trauma connected in any way with our sexuality and physical expression can lead to sexual challenges such as shutting down sexual exploration. It can lead to the inability to have an orgasm, disconnecting or dissociation during sex, fear of being vulnerable and emotional shut down when faced with the possibility of sex or even a discussion of sex. Sexual abuse can lead to the survivor connecting sexual expression – which could be sexual expression of any kind – with shame, disgust and fear. Sexual expression can also bring up traumatic memories they wish to avoid. This reaction can block the body's ability to relax, feel safe and enjoy being touched, even if the woman is safe, alone and touching herself. People who experienced abuse as a child often realize years later that they missed out on natural teenage sexual exploration and experimentation and have some catching up to do.

For some sexual abuse survivors their experience of arousal and orgasm during the abuse can be a particularly significant concern. This becomes confusing in the face of neuro-scientific research tells us that in order to climax, the fear center of the brain needs to shut down and we need to be mentally relaxed. Lots of people, whether they have a vagina or penis, have experienced not being able to get aroused or have an orgasm due to feeling stressed or feeling pressure to perform. But how does this make sense when the occurrence of orgasms during sexual abuse proves that to not always be the case?

The physical occurrence of an orgasm during sexual abuse is due to a neural loop between the genitals and the spinal cord which doesn't even involve our emotions or thoughts. Rest assured, if you have experienced this, it does not mean you wanted or enjoyed the experience. It was just your body's arousal response that happened at a purely physical level as a result of the stimulation. To learn more about this topic, the TED talk 'Unwanted Arousal' by Emily Nagoski explains this phenomena with a strong message of empowerment and reclaiming confidence in our arousal.

Having an experienced therapist and a safe space to heal past traumas and resulting fears connected with sex can be highly beneficial. Someone who has experienced abuse may also find they benefit from specific help to build self-esteem and self-worth, learn how to set boundaries, let their guard down to be emotionally open with a partner and themselves, recognize and act on early warning signs and create a safe attachment with a long term partner. I know this sounds like a lot, and it may sound overwhelming when reading it like this, but each aspect is linked and you will notice how making positive tweaks in one area builds strength and confidence in others. Also, I'm presenting a wide range of ideas for potential therapeutic focus here and not everyone will require help with each of these areas.

You can also start the healing process with specialist self-help books such as: *The Sexual Healing Journey: A Guide for Survivors of Sexual Abuse* by Wendy Maltz or books that focus on healing from the specific type of abuse you experienced. However, I really want to encourage working one-on-one with a therapist you trust to explore your individual and unique emotions, thoughts, beliefs and behaviors as it can make the journey of claiming your body and sexuality back so much easier having someone provide professional support along the way.

Part of the overall process of healing and feeling safe with sexual exploration is gained by setting some clear boundaries around sex and becoming very clear within yourself about what you do and don't feel comfortable doing, and with whom. Remind yourself that you don't owe anyone anything when it comes to your body and your sexuality, and that the journey of discovery and reclaiming your sexuality is yours to choose when and if you wish to do so.

I strongly encourage you to take an attitude of compassionate curiosity with your self-exploration as well as take your time and ensure you are giving yourself lots of self-care throughout the whole discovery process. There is no rush. Take your time. Find someone you trust to talk to about your discoveries if you wish and consider journaling so you have a place where you can collect your thoughts, realizations and progress. And at any time you feel discomfort, allow yourself to take a break or stop until another day. You can work through the general exercises in this book as well as the following "Sensate Focus" exercises that you might find are a good place to start.

Religious guilt

It's unfortunate that many of the women who come to me with psychological issues to do with sexuality, from painful sex to discomfort talking about it with their partners, also refer to having had a strict religious upbringing, which included installing negative beliefs about sex and sexuality. Some teachings that are passed down directly or indirectly through religion include:

– Sex is something that 'should' only occur between a husband and wife

– Masturbation and touching yourself intimately is dirty/naughty/wrong/sinful
– Homosexuality and bisexuality is sinful
– Sex shouldn't be enjoyable
– Good Catholic girls don't think about sex
… and so on. Can you recall the messages you received from your religion?

One suggestion for breaking free of negative messages is to look deeper into the religious texts and various interpretations. Firstly, if you follow the teachings of the Christian Bible, let's start with there being no direct reference to masturbation in the Bible. The online magazine Today's Christian Woman covers this in the article by Louis McBurney, which answers the question *Is Masturbation a Sin?* with a clear no. Allowing masturbation as part of sexual intimacy, as interpreted in the article, might satisfy some. However, it doesn't go so far as to fully encourage masturbation by oneself or in a non-marital relationship.

One overarching message that many Christians can relate to is the following: Beyond all of the micro-details of the teachings, God is said to be omnibenevolent, omniscient and omnipotent (all good, all knowing and all powerful). With this in mind, you could speak to your God; specifically connecting with these qualities. If God is all of these things, then how do you think God feels about you loving and appreciating the body you have been born with? Is it possible that these religious messages are actually the opinion of humans rather than from God?

In therapy and/or through journaling you could explore the early negative messages you received about your body as well as who it was that was teaching you them. Open your mind and heart to the underlying desires behind masturbation for you. Ask yourself how it benefits you, what you seek in learning and experiencing and how this might impact on your life and relationships and comfort with your sexuality and body. If you are seeking professional guidance, you could discuss your thoughts and feelings with a therapist who shares your faith, or you could directly ask God during prayer.

As you take the journey of finding a path that connects both your religious faith and your desire for full sexual expression, be comforted in knowing that you are not alone. Reconciling religious teachings and upbringing with one's adult beliefs and desires is a common path walked by those brave enough to take it.

This exploration and journey of discovery is obviously not limited to Christians. Whatever your religion, first notice if there are areas in which the religious teachings you've grown up with clash with your sexual desires and practices. There might not be any clashes, in which case that's great, because that will make expressing your sexual self much easier. However, if there are clashes, note what they are and then start taking a closer look. Take your time and consult multiple sources for expert opinions and interpretations of the religious texts.

Hopefully you will be able to find peace and connection between your spiritual and sexual world. And if your journey leads you to conclude that the clash is insurmountable, I encourage you to seek support from friends and/or a therapist who can help you figure out your next steps. These could be anything from an internal shift in your religious beliefs to choosing to engage or not engage in certain behaviors. The key in moving forward is that the choice is coming from within and that you allow for the processing of any emotions such as grief, guilt and shame, letting go, and strengthening your sense of identity and belonging.

Painful sex history

Painful sex – whether due to psychological or physical reasons or a combination of both – is something that can reduce a woman's interest in sex and being touched. The idea of continuing sexual exploration in the hope of reaching orgasm can feel scary, discouraging or confronting after a painful sex experience.

Painful sex is experienced by women at various times in their lives due to all sorts of reasons and doesn't have to mean the end of your sex life. In fact, often it's just a sign that something is happening that you hadn't otherwise noticed. The first step is to stop doing anything that causes the pain. Pushing through pain can lead to much more complicated issues and also set up a mind-body loop between sexual touch and pain. In some cases it can even lead to the condition of vaginismus (when the pelvic floor muscles involuntarily tense up and may hinder penetration).

The next step is to get your thinking cap on and explore whether the pain is due to something happening with the skin, nerves, muscles, hormones, medication side effects, or a combination of these. Unfortunately many doctors are untrained in identifying the many possible causes of the pain. So you can really help yourself here by noticing any details of the symptoms, when the pain happens and when it doesn't. Notice for example if it is painful to wipe after going to the toilet, if underwear rubbing against your vulva is painful, whether any regular movement such as walking or sitting hurts, whether penetration is possible and pain free – from tampons or a finger compared to something wider like a penis or vibrator. Collect this data as it will help you narrow down the possible cause and ultimately find the treatment.

The book, *Healing Painful Sex* by Deborah Coady and Nancy Fish is an excellent resource which covers a wide range of conditions. It can really help in the process of identifying the condition/s based on your symptoms. If you have a sex clinic or sex therapist in your area definitely inquire with them or with a pelvic floor physiotherapist or gynecologist. Write or call to make contact, let them know what you have discovered and ask them if this is something they can help with. If the health system operates differently in your country, your first port of call might be your regular doctor who can then refer you to the appropriate specialist. The clearer you are about how and when the pain occurs, the more you're helping them successfully identify the cause. This step is all about diagnosing any physical causes and sometimes requires a number of interventions depending on what it is.

Whatever your experience, ensure you get clarification and treatment. Painful sex issues often require persistence with seeking answers as well as patience and dedication to treatment and homework. There may be a simple answer and treatment, but in some cases it is a more complex path.

You can turn this situation around by seeing it as an opportunity to rethink and re-explore pleasurable physical and sexual sensations. Bring your masturbation play and sex play with a partner back to basics such as touching areas that aren't associated with pain and taking things slowly. Think of all the various sexual activities you can still do and use this time to open up your repertoire and any restricting beliefs about what sex and masturbation 'should be' like. You could also enjoy exploring more of your mental fantasies while you get treatment. Above all, be kind with yourself and allow your body to heal.

If it is discovered that there is a psychological aspect to the pain, then work with a therapist trained in helping retrain the mind and disconnect the body's fear response. If you have been experiencing vaginismus, you might find my other book *Stop Painful Sex: Healing from Vaginismus* useful as well as working with a pelvic floor physiotherapist, who can guide you through using dilators as well as releasing tension through trigger point massage.

Whatever the cause and treatment you end up pursing, you can also support yourself during this time by practicing mindfulness and deep breathing to activate the parasympathetic nervous system; use lubrication during any intimate touch; calm your mind and body with relaxing music; create a comfortable space to re-explore sexual touch where you feel at ease and in control, able to set the pace and stop if you want.

Limiting beliefs and negative associations with masturbation and sexual expression

When you think of masturbation do you automatically associate it with positive or negative feelings? What words come to mind? If it's only positive ones then that's great! You can skip this part. But even if you only have a hint of negativity associated with masturbation it can be worthwhile to consider where that might have come from.

Reflect for a moment on the messages you receive about masturbation from the media (all sources, online as well as print), family and friends, and the society you live in. Negative associations can be a result of current messages and/or messages from the past that we picked up during childhood or youth. Therefore it can be worthwhile to reflect on messages you have received throughout your life. Often people will have one or more memories that stand out as significant moments when beliefs were formed.

The process of writing can help reveal and clarify these

messages and memories. We can sometimes discover more in doing this than just thinking things through in our head. In addition, bringing these messages out into the open can be a positive step of taking back control over what we choose to believe about sex and sexuality. Further processing and healing can also come from metaphorically releasing unhelpful messages in a ritual. How to do a ritual of release, you ask? There are many ways, but a couple of my favorite methods are to either burn the piece of paper you have written the old messages on or bury it. Both methods are an act of letting go of the messages contained on the paper and sending them back to where ever they came from. You could also write the messages onto a paper lantern at night and let it go. You can get really creative with the method of how you want to release the message/s.

It can be powerful to start and end a ritual with a moment of mindfulness. Here are some ideas of how you can complete this ritual (feel free to adapt it and create a ritual that works for you).

Time to play:

<u>A ritual of release</u>

Give yourself time to do this ritual. You might like to light a candle, play music, say a prayer or be somewhere in nature. Identify the negative associations and write them down. Reflect on the source of these messages and write that down as well. Take three deep breaths. Mentally send out a message of appreciation to the source, and thank them for whatever positive intention they might have had. Let them know the message is theirs and you are now giving it back to them. An example of this could be: "Thank you Mom for trying to protect me. I know you thought you were helping me. But these negative messages and beliefs have only held me back from fully loving myself and being happy. These beliefs don't belong to me. They belong to you and I release them back to you now." Now take the paper with the message/s written on it and burn it (of course, while being safe with fire!)

Another example of releasing messages would be burying them in the ground while saying something like: "These messages about my body and my sexuality do not belong to me. They are messages from people who did not know me and who came from a different time with different beliefs, that have not supported my growth or well-being. I bury these messages now and with them any power they have had over me. I give them back to the universe to be broken down and recycled by nature. With this I let go of these old beliefs and create space for growth and acceptance."

At this point some people find it useful to take a moment to choose their own new positive and supportive messages and beliefs. If you do this, find words that resonate with you deeply and make you feel good about yourself. Ensure that the wording is positive. Instead of choosing what something isn't or what you don't want, for example, "I am not ashamed about my sexuality" (which makes us focus on the shame), you could instead choose "I embrace my sexuality". Some other examples of positive sex beliefs and messages are:

– I allow my sexuality to shine
– Sex is something I allow myself to enjoy
– Sex is pleasurable and fun
– I accept my sexuality fully and completely
– I am a sexual being
– Sexual expression is healthy

Rituals and metaphoric processes can be powerful. If my ideas don't connect with you, craft your own letting-go ritual that has personal meaning for you. Another option is being guided through a mental letting-go process in hypnotherapy. This can support change at the subconscious level.

Sensate Focus exercises to help overcome psychological challenges

Originally developed by Masters and Johnson in the 1970's to help couples with performance anxiety, Sensate Focus exercises are still a useful tool for someone who has had negative sexual experiences. Designed to reduce anxiety, increase self-awareness and sexual response, and remove any expectations of outcomes, Sensate Focus exercises also help bring our attention back into the here and now rather than dissociating and create a safe space for sexual exploration.

Historically, this was a model for heterosexual couples working through stages of increasing sexual touch and ultimately ending in intercourse. In an updated inclusive approach, regardless of the couple's genders or sexual orientation, exercises start with non-genital touch and work towards a full expression of sex (whether that does or doesn't include vaginal penetration).

Originally used as part of an intense two week therapy program with daily appointments, the exercises can be incredibly beneficial even when done in your own time and pace. Having regular connection with your body is the important bit, so it's helpful to prioritize doing the exercises every couple of days. Here is an adapted form of the Sensate Focus exercises for use as an individual.

Time to play:

Stage one: Non-genital touch – 15 minutes

Without touching your breasts or genitals, explore the sensations of touch over your entire body. As the name implies, your aim during this exercise is simply to notice and focus on sensations rather than aim for any specific outcome. Do this by noticing any temperature differences, textures (e.g. smooth, soft, hairy, prickly, goosebumps), sounds (e.g. as you run your fingers across your scalp, along your hair, against your ear), the location of the touch (following it in your mind), and what the touch feels like as you use more or less pressure or short or long strokes. If your mind starts to wander during the exercise, simply bring it back to the sensations you are feeling. Remember to touch both the front and back of your body, and you may have to change your position to allow this.

Stage two: Include genital touch – 15 minutes

Once you feel comfortable with stage one (which might be after one, two, ten or more times), you can move on to the next stage. This is the same as stage one, with genital and breast touching added. Continue to focus on sensations rather than aiming to create pleasure. If you do find yourself getting turned on by your touch – which might happen and is totally fine – just notice, but don't act upon it (by seeking to give yourself an orgasm, for example). You could imagine that you have gained the sensation of touch for the first time in your life. As a result, you are exploring what it feels like to feel without judgement or purpose, focusing only on the sensory, sensual and tactile experience.

Stage three: Guiding the touch – 15 minutes

After you are comfortable with full body sensate focusing, you can bring more awareness to pleasure into the exercise. Again, this might be after a number of times doing the stage one and two exercises. In the original couples' version, this stage is where the person being touched starts to give their partner feedback on their preference of touch by placing their hand on top of their partners and then guiding their hand to show where they like a firmer or softer touch, or longer or shorter strokes or circular movements. The aim is still exploration of sensual rather than sexual touch.

Doing this as an individual, you can now focus on noticing what type of touch you prefer as you explore your whole body. Notice where you enjoy a softer, feather light touch and where you enjoy a firmer touch. Notice also the difference between touching with your fingertips compared to using the palm of your hand.

Continue moving around the body, without staying on any particular spot. If near the end of this stage you find that you are in an aroused state, you can proceed to direct sexual touch. This is optional and only suggested if you feel comfortable to proceed.

Stage four: Full sexual expression – 15 minutes

In this final stage you can explore full sexual expression. With the aim still on sensory exploration, you can now open up the exercise to include any sex toys you would like to explore in this sensory way or continue with just your hands. Full exploration and sexual expression is 'allowed' and encouraged at this stage.

Continue to keep the framework in mind. Couples doing this are instructed to do "sensory intercourse" rather than sexual intercourse (take a moment to consider the difference). It is important that you also take your time rather than try to rush things to a predetermined outcome.

The aim is that, by the time you have worked your way through these four stages, you have become attuned to the many variations of touch you find pleasurable, that you are able to bring your attention into the moment during touch, and can focus on the different sensations that your skin and hair provide you with as you are touching yourself. In addition, you will have learned more about the different sensations you can give yourself through altering the pressure, speed and length of your strokes and size of your movements.

Taking the time to regularly practice attuning to your physical sensations in a safe environment where you are 100% in charge will also have helped you on an emotional and psychological level.

Variations: If you prefer, you can begin by doing each of these exercises while clothed before moving onto an unclothed version.

The use of massage oil or lubrication can be used as an additional way to explore the different feelings and sensations of touch.

10. Boosting body acceptance

Feeling comfortable with and accepting our bodies helps us relax in the way the body and mind need in order to reach orgasm. Body acceptance also helps sexual intimacy with others feel more enjoyable, because we're not worrying about how we look or what the other person is thinking about our body. It's one less thing to be thinking about, and thus we are more likely to be able to focus on the experience and stay present with the sensations we're feeling.

Women report that body acceptance gives them more freedom to express their desires, direct their partner to do more or less of something through guiding their hand or through words, body movements or other verbal or non-verbal communication. And not having body acceptance makes all of that much harder.

Masturbation and other acts of treating our bodies with love and care can help our thoughts and emotions about our bodies become more positive and self-accepting.

But first, what does body acceptance mean to you? When I consider this question, I think of embracing and appreciating my unique, physical self regardless of how it compares to others and even how it compares with the way I looked when younger. But what about you? What does body acceptance mean to you?

So many women aren't happy with the way they look. They think the grass is greener on the other side. They want curly or straight hair, bigger or smaller breasts, to be taller or shorter, more or less curves and more or less weight. It seems like a never-ending struggle of comparing ourselves to others and wishing we looked different.

Beauty, however, is extremely fickle. It's really helpful to realize this if you want to embrace your body and your unique self. In order to truly accept our bodies, most of us will have to work against the messages of whatever our society currently views as beautiful, because only a percentage of us will match the current trend. In the Western world, as we're bombarded with heavily filtered and altered bodies in advertising, porn and social media, women are currently plumping things up from lips to breasts and bums while seeking to tone everything else. It hasn't always been like this though.

Ancient Greece (700-480 BC) and around 1400-1700 AD are just two well known time periods when a fuller figure was the epitome of beauty. You were considered hot if you had a soft stomach as well as large breasts and hips. Like they are now, big buttocks and breasts were also celebrated back in the 1930s and 1950s. Yet in the 1920s, 1960's and 1990s a thin, sometimes extremely thin body was promoted. While we might seek muscled limbs and abs now, the corset at times made the preferred waist one that was cinched in tightly. Even as we reflect on current trends, there are multiple and contrasting 'ideals'. Do you see how crazy this is? If you were to live forever, you'd be trying to gain and lose weight and muscles, and completely reshape your body every couple of decades just to try to keep up with the current trend. It's madness!

I find it absurd that women are told they should look a particular way that so often has nothing to do with the body they've been born with. Wouldn't it be great is we just aimed for overall well-being and healthy body function instead?

Start by mentally pushing pause whenever you find yourself comparing your body with someone else's. Remind yourself that what makes a body's shape and size attractive is a trend-based thing. It's as superficial as whether our trousers are currently skinny or wide; hip-grazing or buttoned to the waist, or whether we're even wearing trousers or not. Start loving the body you have, treat it nicely and if you're not quite there yet, be patient with yourself as you learn how to.

This shifting trend of different looks also affects how we view pubic hair and vulvas. Pubic hair has gone through trends over the years, ranging from full bush to fully removed. At times it's been viewed as unsightly and at other times celebrated as beautiful and natural.

In the past, cultures around the world have treated pubic hair in different ways. Widespread pubic hair removal (and general hair removal) in the Western world didn't really become a common thing until closer to modern times. While Gillete brought out its first razor for women back in 1915 coinciding with rising hemlines and sleeves, the Brazilian didn't become a well known option until it featured on Sex and the City in 2000. The keeping or removal of pubic hair is thus also a matter of the dominant trend of the time and place you live in.

What about the vulva itself? Once again, the acceptance of genital differences is something that depends on

114

beliefs and messages from society. We've still got places in the world where female genital mutilation is performed, despite an international outcry and campaigns for girls' rights. And yet we also have women getting labiaplasty, not because it has been deemed medically necessary for comfort, (which is extremely rare) but simply for looks. So many people rate their vulva as abnormal simply because they have only seen a very limited range. Often the preferences originate from mainstream porn where labia may have been small, pale and hairless (and sometimes even bleached).

What thoughts have come up for you as we've reflected on the history of hair removal, body shape trends and societal messages? Take a moment to think about your body and the culture in which you live in. For most women, body acceptance is a journey that takes time and effort. So let's get started!

Time to play:

<u>Messages</u>

Grab a sheet of paper or page in your journal and write down the current year and country in which you live. Fill the page with all the messages you have received about how a female 'should' look in your here and now. What is currently considered attractive? What, if any, messages do you receive about body hair, pubic hair and vulvas? Notice also where and who these messages come from. Is it friends, partners, family, the media, advertising or social media?

On a new page, now write your name and "My body, my choice". Fill the page with the beliefs you choose now to have about your body. What do you want to claim as attractive? What messages do you want to send to yourself? What does your body need to hear from you to feel attractive and accepted by you? Reframe what you have until now seen as negative with a new appreciation and keep sending yourself these new messages. Instead of heavy thighs you could see strong thighs, reframe a wobbly stomach to a cuddly stomach, 'too big' labia to luscious labia. Create a self-love and body appreciation list and keep adding to it over time. Learn from others in the body positivity movement and keep asking yourself: How else can I rename and reclaim my body?

See more vulvas and bodies

Start learning about this by seeking out body-positive books like *Womanhood,* which includes photos of vulvas and stories from 100 women and online vulva galleries like the labia library and Hilde Atalanta's vulva artwork. *Bare Reality* is another body positivity book, which focuses on breasts. *Bare Reality* and *Womanhood* are both by Laura Dodsworth. Another great resource to check out for building body acceptance is Mandi Lynn's TEDx Wellington talk titled 'Every Body is a Treasure' available online.

From looks to function

How about a gentle reminder about what your body is actually designed for. On another sheet, focus on the things you are grateful for about your body. How does your body help you on a daily basis? List all the things you can think of that your body does and can do for you. From helping you get nutrients from the food you eat, keeping you alive by pumping blood through your body, shivering when cold, to movement and touch and all that your senses allow you to experience about the world around you. Think of as many things as you can that you appreciate your body doing for you – from the top of your head to the soles of your feet.

Mindful scan for body acceptance

I suggest you record the following exercise so you can close your eyes and listen back to it. That will probably be a lot easier than reading it at the same time as trying to do it. As you read it, speak in a very slow voice and make pauses in between each idea or sentence. You might also like to play some relaxing music in the background to include in the recording.

Sit or lie down in a comfortable position. Take a moment to notice your surroundings. Take note of any colors around you... and any movement. And notice the rise and fall of your breath as you take this moment to just be.

You might like to close your eyes as you bring your attention to the top of your head. Scan your attention down through your face and let your jaw relax.

Notice, as you scan through your body, if there are any thoughts or feelings that come to mind about each body part. As you notice these thoughts and feelings, allow yourself to just breathe and observe it in the same way that you could watch a cloud gently float across the sky. You don't have to try to change the thought or react to it in any way. Just notice it from a distance – "oh there's a thought ... ah yes, that emotion" and continue in your scanning while continuing to notice the rise and fall of your breath.

Next, bring your attention to your neck... and to your shoulders. Scanning and flowing your focus down your upper arms and your chest. Just observing. Continuing down through your core and lower arms and hands. Scanning down through your pelvis and thighs. Flowing your attention down the rest of your legs and all the way to the tips of your toes. Allowing any thoughts and emotions to drift by like clouds in a calm blue sky.

Take a few deep breaths as you rest your attention at the

soles of your feet. *(Allow some time for the breaths here)*.

Now bring your attention gently back to the top of your head. Imagine a healing light above you. Allow this healing light to flow into you sending loving acceptance through your entire being. With your breath, flow this healing light down through your head and face... down your neck and shoulders. Allow it with every breath to flow further down... filling every cell with loving acceptance and healing. Flow it through your chest and core. All the way down your arms to the tips of your fingers. Flow the healing light through your pelvis and legs. Soothing you all the way down to the soles of your feet.

Rest a while in this healing light. Bathe in loving acceptance and notice any thoughts just like the clouds that can pass gently by. Feel your breath and allow it to continue sending this loving acceptance throughout every part of you.

(After a couple of minutes)... Gently reorient yourself back to the sounds around you. And with three deep breaths in and out, bring your attention fully back to the here and now and open your eyes.

– *End of exercise*

You might like to write down or illustrate any learnings or realizations that you gained during this exercise.

Love your body

The more you love and treat your body as that of a sexual goddess, the more you can step out of your head, away from self-judgment and into sexual ecstasy and fulfillment. If the word goddess doesn't resonate with you, pick another one that does. Here are some options: Sexual or sensual being, enlivened, sexually attuned and sexy self. But you don't actually need a name for it. I'm talking about connecting with your sexual interest and drive, curiosity, willingness to play, embodying and embracing your body and all that you can experience with it.

Plan dates with your body where you treat yourself with physical love and affection.

You could, for example, draw a self-portrait of yourself in full goddess mode. The image doesn't have to be realistic. Mine would include shells and flowers in my hair. I'd be draped with energy swirls and have a strong, spiritual connection with the ocean because I love the beach and nature. But that's me... what about you? What would your goddess self look like?

Do you have a bath in your home? If you do, then another way you could treat your body with love is to take a bath with that intention in mind. As you lie back in the warm water, imagine the warmth soothing your muscles and also melting away any harsh judgment. Just as you did in the previous exercise, imagine love flowing all the way through your body. What color would you give love flowing through your body like that? Also, enjoy savoring the sensations of floating in the water and feeling the water wash over your chest and breasts. Give yourself permission to claim your sexual and sensual sensations even in the simple moment of having a bath. If you don't have a bathtub, you can do this in the shower – flowing your love through your body as the water washes over you and noticing the delicious body sensations. You could also do this in a lake, river or ocean on a warm summer's day.

Also, remember you can treat yourself and your body with love through the clothes you wear and the way you move your body, with any products you use on your skin and touch you give yourself.

Notice other ideas that come to you as you explore the embodiment of your sexual self. We are all unique in our sexuality and how we perceive and experience it. Therefore, give yourself permission to look for ways that will work for you.

Healing light – 'May I feel loved' meditation

This is another guided meditation that you might like to record and play back so you can follow the imagery without having to read at the same time. Make sure to read very slowly and include breaks in between the sentences. In the second part of the meditation, which contains suggestions for acceptance and growth, you might have some sentences you'd like to add that ring true for you personally.

Start by getting into a comfortable position. Connect with an intention of sending your body love and acceptance. Bring your awareness to your breath and feel your chest and belly expand as you breathe in… and… out. Take a deep breath in… and exhale. Take another deep breath in and let your muscles relax as you slowly breathe out again. And take a third deep breath in and allow yourself to relax deeper as you breathe out slowly. As you breathe deeply, connect with your heart and the desire to embrace your sexual self.

Now gently allow your breath to settle in its own time. You might like to experiment with the duration of the in and out-breath for a little while as you find a comfortable rhythm or you can allow it to naturally settle by itself.

Bring your attention to the rest of your body. Feel supported by the chair you are sitting in or the surface you are resting on. Pay attention and really notice the sensation of being supported.

As you allow yourself to rest, imagine a soft swirl of healing white light resting above your head. With your next breath out, allow the light to start gently flowing through your body from the top of your head to the tips of your toes. With every breath let it flow further and deeper throughout your body. Let it flow to your pelvis and shine from deep within. Imagine the healing light resting there and bathing you in healing light. Let it grow like an unfolding flower, blossoming from your pelvis and expanding its energy in a great circle of light. Imagine it soothing and softening any self-judgment, shame, pressure, or sadness that you might have been carrying about yourself or your body. As the healing light expands throughout and beyond your body, imagine it softening those old feelings about yourself as it radiates from within you. As you continue to radiate this healing light, you can be curious about what happens to that old self-judgment.

You might feel that it is dissolving or disappearing. Perhaps it melts away or gets released more and more with your out breaths. Be curious how you could imagine letting go of any self-judgment. Or perhaps you want to hold on to it a little longer and just let it soften and fade by itself. What feels right for you now?

As you connect with this healing light, send yourself positive messages:

May I feel loved.

May I feel safe.

May I enjoy my body, my sensuality and sexuality.

With each exploration and step on my journey, I choose to shed old beliefs and judgments that come from others or my past. I let go of that which does not bring me joy.

I let go of pain and judgment from the past and allow my sexuality to awaken and grow.

I allow myself to see and feel my beauty.

I allow myself to start embodying my sexual self as I choose.

I give myself permission to enjoy sex.

I give myself permission to enjoy my body, my sensuality and sexuality.

I allow myself to explore getting aroused.

I accept my sexual self.

I take responsibility for my own sexual pleasure.

I am open to learning more about myself.

It is okay to feel and enjoy pleasure.

I am a sexual being.

I let myself approach sexual experiences with playfulness and curiosity.

I listen to my body; its needs and desires.

May I feel loved.

May I feel safe.

May I feel content.

May I feel pleasure.

Feel these messages reach deep within you. Allow them to settle and take a moment to notice how these new thoughts and decisions resonate with where you are on your journey.

Connect once more with the healing light. Feel its energy in your body. Feel how its source is now you.

Know that you can at any time reconnect with self-healing and self-love by taking a moment to focus back on this energy and anything else that has stood out for you in this experience.

You might like to take a few deep breaths and stretch as you bring your attention back to your present surroundings and open your eyes with a sense of curiosity about how you will continue on this journey.

Resting hand

In doing the previous meditation exercises, you will have learned and practiced sending loving energy through your body. This exercise is self-guided and will allow you to focus and direct your attention to the various parts of your body as you wish.

You may choose to prepare for this exercise by either doing something relaxing of your choice or by listening to one of the meditations above. You might like to play relaxing music while you do this or you might enjoy silence. You can do this exercise clothed or naked – whatever feels most comfortable for you right now. Because I'm going to suggest that you touch your vulva, lying on your back might be the preferable position, but be your own judge and do what works best for you.

For this exercise, you're going to place a hand on a body part and direct your attention there in a loving and curious way. People can be very disconnected from their body and really benefit from tuning into it in a mindful way. You can choose where you start and what parts you include. Here are a couple of examples:

Place your hand on your breast. Notice the initial sensations and what stands out for you. You don't have to move your hand or caress the breast in any way. Simply rest your hand there and feel the sensations on the skin of your hand and also feel the sensations on your breast. Gently notice if any thoughts or emotions come up and just as you have done in previous exercises, acknowledge the thought or emotion and allow it to float away like a cloud as you notice what else you sense. If your breast has been operated on or changed in any way including after breastfeeding, then notice anything that comes up about that experience and allow that also to drift in and out of your focus. You can always redirect your attention back to your breath. You can also send loving energy through your hand to your breast. Your goal is simple: connect in with the physical sensations with loving energy. When you feel ready, change sides and place a hand on your other breast.

As mentioned, I invite you to take the time to do this with multiple areas around your body. When you do the exercise with the vulva, relax your legs so that you can cup it with your hand. Once again, your goal is to simply rest your hand and tune in with this part of your body. Take deep breaths. Feel the sensation on the skin of your vulva and also feel the sensation on the skin of your hand. Notice details like temperature and softness. Send love to your vulva. Notice any thoughts and emotions. Allow them to just be as you continue feeling your breath and the sensations in your body as you send love to this part of yourself. When you feel ready to move on to the next area of your body, simply move on.

Each time you do this exercise with a part of your body you are bringing your conscious awareness to it and helping your awareness of physical sensations grow. With every chosen mindful moment like this, you are inviting this part of your body to awaken. At the same time, you are creating and strengthening neural pathways of body awareness and safe, pleasurable touch.

PART TWO: PHYSICAL STIMULATION TECHNIQUES

External stimulation techniques

1. Erogenous zones

Think back to the exercise earlier in the book in which you explored your erogenous zones. What areas of your body did you notice sparked sexual arousal or even just felt really good to touch? Masturbating doesn't have to focus on your pelvic area. You can make creating pleasure and exploring your individual sensuality as a full-body expression.

So approach your body anew. Play with different types of touch. Soft, gentle strokes and tickles as well as deeper massage. Use your hands, fingertips, a feather, vibrator, electric toy, an ice cube – playfully and lovingly explore in whichever ways you want.

Some erogenous zones you might like to explore (aside from the obvious ones you've already discovered) are the inner thighs, inner wrists and arms, stomach, ears, lips, neck, perineum, palms of your hands and your feet.

Time to play:

Embellished touch

Next time you masturbate, take a few minutes at the start to spark sensations throughout your entire body. Caress your skin lightly and find delight in your erogenous zones. Breathe deeply as your body awakens to your touch.

Use this pleasurable touch of your erogenous zones as a foundation to build on. Once you feel arousal building, then continue with your chosen masturbation style. This might be when you get out a vibrator, stroke around the clitoris with a finger, or grind against something. As arousal builds through the excitement and plateau phases before orgasm, combine your favorite masturbation techniques with erogenous zone stimulation as an embellishment. Think of it like a cherry on top – it might not be the main flavor but it enhances the experience due to simultaneously stimulating more nerves associated with pleasure.

2. Fingers

The way a lot of females start out (and often continue) masturbating is by using their fingers. Many women reach orgasm this way. Touching yourself with your fingers is a simple way to learn what type of touch you like. You can use your own saliva to moisten your fingers and vulva or use a good quality lubricant, which will give a silky slipperiness. After a while of continual touch, or if you were already turned on when you started playing, you'll naturally produce your own lubrication.

Try out using one or both of your hands. Mastering self-pleasure and orgasm this way ensures you can take your skill with you wherever you are and you don't have to worry about anyone hearing the buzz of a vibrator or having to transport your toys with you when traveling. A one-handed technique may feel more relaxed and simple while using two hands can increase pleasure through touching different areas at the same time. You won't know how it is for you until you've tried it.

Time to play:

Extended lines

Place either your index or middle finger above your clitoris pointing down with the rest of your hand resting on your mons pubis. With your chosen finger, make long strokes that go from the top of the clitoris, down between the labia, a little into the vagina and then back up. For this movement, maintain skin contact along the whole of the finger as you rub along the entire length.

This movement mimics the up and down grinding motion of the Coital Alignment Technique described earlier and can also (along with most finger-based techniques) be enjoyed using a toy or vibrator.

Two handed

With one hand, circle or softly rub around the clitoral hood and head. At the same time, stroke around the vaginal opening.

Continue circling the clitoris with a finger or fingers from one hand while running a finger along the ridges of your inner labia with the other hand. Keep exploring with the two handed approach – the dominant hand making the core movement that turns you on and the other adding to the sensations.

Clitoris

The clitoris is the most commonly chosen spot for self-pleasuring (chosen by 73% of women according to the Hite Survey). Touching this area is a 'go-to' method for many, because the clitoris is ultra sensitive and easy to access. Stimulating yourself by touching your clitoris is a good place to start if you are new to masturbating, want to learn how to pleasure yourself sexually or are not sure where to start.

Because direct touch of the clitoris can become too intense or even painful (especially after an extended length of time or harder rubbing), self-pleasuring has the bonus of giving you feedback along with full control. You can instantly adapt intensity, speed and pressure as needed at any time. Those surveyed in the Hite Survey generally reported a technique of gentle, sustained movement – first caressing with a gentle motion, then increasing speed as arousal heightens. 'Rapid agitation' of the exact spot that gives the most pleasure is the way that brings the majority of women to an orgasmic climax.

Variations of touch could include: Rubbing, circling, pressing down, caressing the clitoral hood that covers the head or touching it indirectly through the labia or through material such as your underwear.

Time to play:

Spot the Sensitivity

Locate your clitoral head at the top of your inner labia. Explore its sensitivity by gently sliding a moistened fingertip over its top and along each side. Notice if you are someone who finds this direct touch pleasurable or too intense.

Contrast this feeling with the sensitivity you feel when

indirectly touching the clitoris – by making soft downward strokes over the hood for example, or by pressing against the head from the outer side of your labia.

Locate your clitoral shaft

As described back in the anatomy section, the clitoris is so much more than just the head or bud that most people think of when they hear the word clitoris or clit. Another external part of the clitoris is the shaft.

Locate the shaft by placing your straightened index and middle fingers on either side of the head (fingers pointing towards your vaginal opening) and press in against and above the head to feel the firmer tissue underneath. This is the shaft. Caress the shaft with a gentle up and down motion, noticing the difference in texture between the clitoral head, the shaft and the very soft labia. The hardness of the head and shaft will depend on how aroused you are. During arousal and the accompanying engorgement, the erectile tissue that is the clitoris will swell and become harder. This more indirect touch of the shaft may be preferable, if you found direct stimulation of the head uncomfortable. You could also play with placing your fingers inside or outside the outer labia to increase or decrease the directness of your touch on the shaft.

Note: Being able to feel the clitoris beyond just the head will be a lot easier once you are aroused and the clitoral tissue is engorged. Therefore, consider masturbating a little before this exercise to really be able to feel the shaft and the difference in sensation when rubbing that instead of the head.

Loop-de-loop

Use one or more fingers to circle your clitoris. Oscillate between small tight circles around the head and wider loops that slide over the clitoral hood and down over your labia. Notice whether you enjoy lighter or firmer pressure.

Vertical strokes

With your index or middle finger, make short strokes along one side of the clitoral hood in an up and down motion. Experiment with your proximity to the hood and head. Start by making your strokes further out to one side so the movement is along the top of the outer labia. Then bring your touch closer to the middle so that you are right up against the side of the hood. Notice whether you enjoy a more direct contact with the clitoris by stroking along the ridge of the hood and over the head. Then move your strokes to the other side, directly alongside the hood and then further out. Continue this motion from side to side and back again.

In addition to an up and down movement, play with doing only the upward strokes or only the downward strokes. Each will feel different. The pressure can also be adapted from firmer touch, which moves the skin tissue with the finger, and super soft strokes, which only lightly graze the surface.

U-spot

Remember, the space running between the labia from clitoral head to the vaginal opening is sometimes referred to as the U-spot. Other times, it refers to just the area around your urethral opening. If your clitoris can get too sensitive during masturbation then try alternating between stroking between the labia and the clitoris. You might also enjoy how giving yourself pauses from clitoral touch allows the pleasurable build-up of tension and physical arousal without over stimulation of the clitoral head. Once when you are fully aroused, you might like to focus on more intense touch of the clitoris.

Time to play:

<u>The wider U</u>

Gently run a lubricated finger along the entire length between your labia. Focus your attention on the silky texture of the skin here. Take your time to draw your fingertip up and down repeatedly but slowly. This move in itself probably wont give you an orgasm but is another way to enhance your sensory experience, awaken additional nerves and increase overall pleasure.

<u>Focus on the U</u>

Here we're taking the definition of the smaller U-spot as being just around the urethral opening. Add lube to your finger and draw soft ovals around the urethra varying from small circles to wider ones. Also experiment with soft up strokes that go from below the urethra, up and over as well as literally stroking a u shape underneath and from side to side of the urethra. As I've mentioned elsewhere, this is a spot that some women find pleasurable and others don't. Therefore, approach it like the rest of the exercises – with curiosity to learn about your body and your pleasure.

Labia (aka lips)

Another area that responds well to touch is the labia. Both inner and outer labia are filled with sensitive nerve endings and blood vessels. As you get aroused, they swell and can be very pleasurable to touch gently, rub along, tug and stroke or massage.

Along with the space between them, caressing your labia can be interchanged with clitoral touch. Using both hands, you could also give yourself multiple sensations by using one hand on the clitoris and the other stroking the labia and U-spot.

Time to play:

Light lines

Draw light lines with a finger along the ridge of your inner labia – along one side then the other and from top to bottom as well as bottom to top. Stroke along the length at the middle of the labia as well as in the fold between inner and outer labia. Try feather-light touch as well as harder strokes that pull the labia along with the finger.

Butterfly wings

With lubricated fingers, spread the inner labia outwards in soft stroking motions. Try one side, then the other as well as both sides at the same time. Make gentle repetitive movements of opening the labia to spread like a butterfly's wings.

Just hold me

There might be times when stroking feels too intense. It might be at the start of your play or post orgasm when you're taking a breather between orgasms. In this case, cupping your vulva with your palm and applying pressure can feel grounding. At the same time it provides a more calming form of stimulation and connection.

If you are practicing genital awareness as part of tuning in to sensations or doing body-focused meditation, vulva cupping in this way can direct your attention and sensitivity to physical sensations as well as your emotional and mental state.

Perineum and perineal sponge

Reaching down even further, you can include the area running from the vaginal opening to the anus in your self-pleasuring. Due to the high amount of nerve endings located here, this is another site of pleasure for many people. Another area that is highly sensitive due to those nerve endings, is the perineal sponge that lies underneath the skin. Simply applying pressure here can be very arousing when combined with other touch. As always, try different strokes and pressure.

Time to play:

<u>Two-handed</u>

While rubbing your clitoris with one hand, reach under your thigh with your other hand to stimulate the perineum and anus. You can stimulate this area by pressing and rubbing. This reach-around method might be difficult for some people due to the length of your arm and torso or flexibility. In this case, it may be easier to stimulate the perineum and anus with a toy or vibrator instead. The anus doesn't produce its own lubrication so add lube to increase pleasure and lessen friction.

3. Vibrators

Using a vibrator is an easy way to heighten pleasure and decrease the time taken to orgasm. Some women worry that using a vibrator on their clitoris will permanently numb the sensitive nerve endings. This is one of those myths that circulate despite the fact that it's not true. Studies have shown that while the nerves can become less sensitive to lighter stimulation after vibrator use, sensitivity returns to normal after a few days. So basically, you have nothing to worry about. If you're still concerned, then just mix up your techniques – use your fingers one day, a vibrator another day – knowing how to pleasure yourself in different ways and having multiple options is a good idea anyway.

The vibrating sensations quickly arouse many people and because it's a foreign item, it's quite different from using your fingers (where you get the simultaneous sensations from touching skin as well as the feeling of the area being touched). A vibrator against your skin regardless of surface texture, produces a completely different sensation from your own skin on skin.

You can use a vibrator externally much in the same way you use your fingers – pressing against or rubbing the clitoris, sliding between the labia, teasing the vaginal opening and running up and down the inner and outer labia. It's simply a matter of trying it all out and finding what feels best for you. Remember what feels good one day might be different from another day!

Time to play:

<u>Sit and grind</u>

Take a comfortable chair you can straddle. Sit on it back to front and lean forward against the backrest for support. Place a towel or cushion underneath you if you require it for comfort. Position a vibrator on the chair directly underneath you with its tip pointing back towards you. Press down against its hard form and rub your pelvis forward and back as you might when straddling someone.

Notice if you prefer the vibrator pointing forward or backward; whether you like rubbing forward up and onto the vibrator, sliding forward off its tip, or sitting with the main shaft directly between your labia and against your clitoris. **Note:** This might only make sense once you're actually doing it!

Enjoy the sensations of grinding against the vibrations as well as pressing against it with pulsing motions.

Anal play

With a lubricated vibrator, slide or hold the vibration against your perineum. Switch between sliding movements, pressing down and pulsing against the perineal sponge. Experiment with using the tip of the vibrator to create focused stimulation as well as placing the vibrator's length between your butt checks so that the vibration also stimulates the anus. Using the tip of the vibrator, you can also circle around the anus and place it directly against the center of the anus itself.

Vibrator as finger replacement

What were your favorite moves in previous exercises in which you were using your fingers for stimulation? Repeat those exercises, but this time use a vibrator at different vibration settings instead of your fingers. Compare which parts of your vulva respond more to the vibrator and which more to your fingers.

Vibrating finger

If you enjoy vibrating sensations, but also want the direct control of movement that comes from using your finger then pop on a finger massager. This little toy slips over your finger to combine the best of both worlds. Explore all the above moves – sliding between your labia, along their length, up and over the clitoris and play with circles, small and wide.

Press and hold

Press a vibrator against your clitoris. Hold it softly against the head. Find out whether you have a preferred side – against the left or right side, or vibrating from above through the hood, from underneath or directly on top. Simply press and hold, find your favorite spot/s then proceed to soft pulses and strokes if desired.

4. Water play

Shower head

The massage setting on your shower head transforms a means of washing into a handy source of sexual pleasure. Experiment with spraying water directly against your clitoris and labia from front on and from above. Adjust the pressure and temperature of the spray to find what feels best (test the temperature first and make sure not to have it too hot). The closer the shower head is to your body, the higher the intensity; the further away the head is, the less intense the stimulation. Start at a low pressure and build up from there, because while the maximum spray intensity may feel great on your back, it might feel more like sandpaper once it's against your clitoris.

Depending on the length of the hose and shower floor or bath length, you can explore standing and sitting or lying for this kind of water play.

A word of caution: Take care not to spray water directly into the vagina as this can upset the healthy vaginal environment. Washing out natural flora can increase the risk of getting an infection from any bacteria that might come from the shower head as well as making the vagina more susceptible to sexually transmitted infections. Water spray into the vagina could also create small tears in the sensitive walls, which in itself can cause inflammation or infection and lead to pain during intercourse. You will also want to avoid spraying water into the urethra for the same reasons.

Time to play:

<u>Variation 1</u>

Take the shower head off it's bracket and set it to the regular spray setting. Start by gently spraying along your inner thighs, around your breasts and along the sides of your torso. Make slow sweeping movements up and down these erogenous zones. At the same time, bring your focus to your breath and any awareness of a growing arousal.

As you become more connected with your bodily sensations, start orbiting your vulva with the soft spray.

Tighten the circular movement as you direct the spray towards the clitoris. Continue by guiding the spray gently up and down your vaginal lips with occasional passing across the clitoris.

If your clitoris is not too sensitive, experiment with focusing the spray directly against the clitoris as your arousal peaks.

Variation 2

Take the experience up a notch by changing the setting to massage spray. Keep the flow pressure low as you repeat the above movements at this more intense setting. Adjust the water pressure as you hold the flow against the clitoral head and notice your preference: direct spray, from above, from each side and from below.

Variation 3

Enjoy the water spray against your clitoral head while holding a dildo or vibrator inside your vagina. Either stand with your legs together to hold the dildo inside or with the hand not holding the shower head, slide the toy in and out while continuing to stimulate your clitoris with the spray.

Jacuzzi

Pressing your vulva against the jets in a Jacuzzi is an easy, albeit very intense, hands-free way to get physically aroused very quickly. This is similar to using the massage option on a shower head, but with less control over the power of the jet's pressure. If you are going to try this, once again be very careful to aim the pressure against the side of your labia and clitoris and not into your vaginal opening or urethra.

Similar to the feeling of reaching climax in the shower, a Jacuzzi orgasm is more intense, because of the full body water immersion and heat against your skin. Some people will find the high pressure of the spray far too intense but if you like using the massage setting in the shower on your clitoris then this might also be something you enjoy.

5. Pressing & rubbing

Tightening of muscles

Doing your pelvic floor muscle exercises while thinking sexual thoughts is a way of creating very enjoyable yet subtle and discrete sexual pleasure. You can also play with tightening and releasing your butt muscles (including the anal sphincter) as well as your thighs to create sexual arousal. You can do this almost anywhere; while brushing your teeth, waiting for a train, or in anticipation of time with a lover.

Time to play:

Just squeeze

Squeeze and imagine lifting up your pelvic floor muscles. Hold and release while taking deep breaths. Replay a sexual experience in your mind or think of a fantasy at the same time as holding and releasing. As the muscles are activated and your attention is drawn to your bodily sensations, imagine you are being stimulated (your choice how) by yourself or someone else.

Awareness

Combining sexual thoughts, tightening of muscles, or manual stimulation with a conscious tuning in to what's going on in your body and your physical responses can be a powerful combination when it comes to arousal. There is a direct link between paying attention to your body's response and increased feelings of being aroused.

Pressing thighs

For the majority of women, just pressing the thighs together is not going to be enough stimulation to reach a high level of arousal, let alone an orgasm. However, it can be part of the movements that you make while pleasuring yourself. For example, you could close your legs and press your thighs together while stimulating your clitoris with your fingers or vibrator.

Don't get too reliant on this position though as it limits your options during sex with a partner. It's a good idea to interchange it with legs open positions and learn how to get aroused and climax with legs both open and closed.

Rubbing against something

This is how many women experience self-pleasuring for the very first time – as children discovering the good feelings they can create in their bodies. It's a good choice for beginners or those who are not yet comfortable about direct hand-to-genital contact. That said, a friend of mine swears by this method as her 'go to' for an easy orgasm on her own.

Time to play:

Pillow as lover

Take a pillow and lie face down with it placed between your legs. You might have to experiment with the firmness of the pillow you use for this or play with folding or rolling it up to create the height and firmness that works for you. An alternative to a pillow is a rolled-up towel.

Next, grind up against the pillow ensuring that your

clitoris is directly rubbing against it. Let your imagination take you into a hot fantasy or simply enjoy the feelings of the grinding motion.

Internal stimulation techniques

A general note about internal stimulation techniques: Some people prefer to 'warm up' with external stimulation first before any kind of penetration. It's through becoming aroused that the vagina becomes lubricated and tissues become engorged and thus more pleasurably sensitive to touch. But don't let that stop you from exploring penetration in the initial stages of arousal if that interests you. Simply be aware that the sensations you feel internally at the start of the arousal process will feel different to the same movements done later and you'll need to use lube unless already aroused.

1. Fingers

Using your fingers to stimulate your vagina is an easy option that requires no extra gadgets. Just add a lubricant (saliva works fine) and you're ready to go. Try simple insertion and withdrawal movements, press up against the vaginal walls, locate and stimulate your G-spot and combine internal touch with external caresses and rubbing.

Time to play:

<u>Entrance only</u>

Insert only one or two thirds of a finger into your vagina. This part of the vagina is generally more sensitive than deeper inside due to a higher concentration of nerve endings near the opening. Make slow and smooth movements as you slide a finger in and out only up to the first or second knuckle. Combine this move with some of the external techniques from earlier, e.g. circling the clitoris, sliding your finger between the labia, around the vaginal opening, and then softly inside.

Deeply flowing in and out

As above, insert a finger into your vagina, but this time deepen the movement to incorporate most of your finger's length. Increase sensations and body awareness by matching penetration with your breath. Breathe in as you slide your finger in, breathe out as you slide it out. Bring focused awareness to the entirety of the movement; the sensations of the skin against your finger, the sensations inside your vagina as well as the rest of your body as you breathe deeply with your movements.

Come hither

'Come hither' is the classic description of the finger movement that stimulates the G-spot. Remember from the earlier anatomy section, the G-spot has a sponge-like, rougher texture than the skin surrounding it.

For this exercise, insert your index or middle finger into your vagina and press up against the anterior wall (front of the body) as you locate this area. Make the beckoning up and along movement in a repetitive motion. To illustrate this movement, think of it as if you are wanting to draw your lubrication from deep within, along your vaginal wall as your beckoning finger brings it to the opening. This can be an enjoyable interlude from clitoral stimulation or done at the same time.

Tapping the G-spot

This is a movement that works to increase sensations as you get closer and closer to orgasm. It can also heighten the intensity of the orgasm itself. Therefore, make sure to try this out when you are really turned on and getting closer to orgasm.

Insert one or two fingers into your vagina and rapidly tap up against your G-spot. Explore tapping against the area softly as well as with more pressure. Also, compare this type of tapping to a firmer pulsing while maintaining skin contact.

2. Vibrators

Essentially a massaging device, vibrators come in a number of shapes and sizes. For internal use, a long phallic-shaped vibrator gives you a lot of options. You can use a basic form to provide the satisfaction of having something for your vaginal muscles to press up against as you get aroused and during the rhythmic contractions of the muscles during an orgasm. You can insert and withdraw it as deep or shallow as you want and the vibration gives the options of additional stimulation whether used internally or externally.

A vibrator is an essential item for many women when it comes to sexual pleasure. In their simplest forms they are affordable and easy to purchase with practically every sex shop offering a wide selection. Vibrators are easy to use and help many women start exploring and learning about their sexuality and arousal process. Remember regardless of how long you normally take to reach orgasm, using a vibrator generally reduces the time to orgasm by half. Expanding your self-pleasuring skills and boosting your comfort with your sexual self also gives you options for increasing passion with a partner.

Some designs have gained popularity due to their multiple functions. One of these is sometimes referred to as 'The Rabbit'. Providing simultaneous stimulation to the clitoris and vagina, a 'rabbit' vibrator has the add-on of 'ears' to the main shaft, which remain outside the vagina and vibrate against the clitoris. This form of vibrator became extremely popular and well-known after featuring on the television show 'Sex and the City' in the late 1990s. Designs for dual stimulation have continued to be improved and fine-tuned since that early model.

Another interesting design in the world of vibrators is when they are given a curved tip for G-spot stimulation. While you can take a regular vibrator and angle it so that it is vibrating against this area, you may find yourself having to regularly adjust it. In contrast, a curved vibrator makes direct G-spot stimulation easier. If you're looking for a discreet option you might like to try a mini vibrator 'bullet' or a vibrator that has the appearance of a lipstick. And for hands-free fun, you can explore using a U-shaped couples' vibrator during solo play.

Time to play:

Low vibrations

This is a useful way to increase pleasure while at the same time practicing focusing your attention on one main source of stimulation. Try it if you find your mind wandering during sex. Insert a vibrator into your vagina and hold it in place while stimulating your clitoris. You can either hold the vibrator with a hand or by pressing your thighs against it. Keeping it at a low vibration has the benefit of bringing awareness to internal sensations that can at the same time hum away in the background. The vibrations will also be waking up the interior parts of your clitoris to boost the good vibes. The task here is to focus enjoying the sensations of the direct touch to the clitoral head.

Inner clitoral stimulation

Once you feel physiologically aroused during masturbation, insert a vibrator into your vagina and stimulate the inner parts of the clitoris. With arousal, the clitoral tissue will have become engorged (aka erect) and thus it will be more easy to feel the internal clitoral bulbs pressing up against the vaginal canal. You wont be able to touch the bulbs internally as directly as you can the clitoral head on the outside, however you can stimulate them through the vaginal walls.

The aroused clitoris engorges in a way that the bulbs 'hug' either side of your vagina. Use a vibrator with a girth that fits comfortably while also being in contact with the vaginal walls. Alternatively, you can use a narrower vibrator and explore angling it to focus its vibrations more against one wall. Note that any G-spot stimulation is also stimulation of the clitoris as it presses in from above where the bulbs and legs meet the top of the clitoris.

With this exercise, the aim is to simply explore and get familiar with your body (in this case with a special focus on the clitoris) and learn more about what does and doesn't feel good for you personally.

Turning on your A-spot

You can increase your own lubrication and get a wider range of sensations leading up to and during your upcoming orgasm by stimulating the A-spot. A long, curved vibrator is recommended for this but you can use a regular one held at an angle. You want to be directing the vibrations high up your anterior wall (past the G-spot).

Firstly, activate awareness of this area by making slow, gentle caresses with the vibrator using an in-and-out movement that also rubs against the G-spot. Once you are feeling strong sensations from this, rest the vibrator inside with the tip against the A-spot. Without any additional movement, take a moment to focus your attention on the physical sensations this creates. With a quiet, meditative mind notice details such as whether it provokes warmth, how far you feel the vibrations inside you and what muscles are getting activated inside. Notice what other reactions are taking place in your body; how you are breathing and whether you are starting to crave touch in other places.

After a couple of minutes, notice how it feels to gently move the vibrator again so that it caresses against this A-spot area and follow your intuition for what you crave next. In addition, notice how much more wet you have become in a short time.

Double vibrations

Take a couple's vibrator such as the We-Vibe with a curved U-shape. Designed with penetrative partner sex in mind, you can enjoy the double sensations it gives on its own. Turn it on and then insert it so that the inside is pressing up against your G-spot and the outside against your clitoral head.

Generally, these vibrators come with a remote control (and sometimes a corresponding phone app) that gives the option of changing mode and intensity without having to press a button on the device itself. If that takes you too much into your head and out of your body, then choose the vibration mode and intensity before inserting it and leave it at the one setting.

Press your thighs together enough to hold the vibrator in place. Now, it's totally up to you what you choose to do as an accompaniment. You could take a seated position or lie on your front and grind against it. You could lie

146

on your back and rock your pelvis or squeeze your thighs to add your own pulsing to increase and decrease pressure. Your hands are also free to caress the rest of your body.

Anal variation: Flip the toy around so the clitoris arm vibrates against your perineum and anus instead. You can either enjoy it just like this or add additional clitoral stimulation with your fingers or another vibrator to maximize stimulation.

Between the lips

Before penetration, build sexual tension with a transitioning move that takes you from external stimulation only to incorporating internal stimulation as well.

Take a regular vibrator and slide it between your labia. Slide it with full skin contact from base to tip so the base rubs against the clit while the tip brushes over the vaginal opening. Add lube if you don't have enough of your own to make this a slippery movement between skin and vibrator.

Slide the vibrator up and down for a while before tipping it up at the end of the stroke to push the tip a little inside the vagina. Rest it back down against the skin and continue the sliding motion. Mix up between the sliding move with shallow penetrations – increasing the depth and frequency of penetration as you desire.

3. Dildos

Regardless of the material it's made of, a dildo is a phallic-shaped object, which is typically used for insertion but can also be used to rub against the skin externally. The key difference between a vibrator and a dildo is that a dildo doesn't vibrate, which is why some people just choose to buy vibrators because they can use them turned on or off. A couple of common uses are to insert them vaginally and hold them inside while squeezing the pelvic floor muscles, or move them in and out repeatedly mimicking intercourse (vaginally or anally). Most commonly for women, dildos are used to create a satisfying feeling of vaginal fullness while the fingers massage the clitoris to orgasm. Added pleasure is experienced due to the muscles inside the vagina having something to contract against in the lead up to and during orgasm.

Dildos come in a wide range of sizes in both width and length. They can be double pronged for simultaneous vaginal and anal penetration and also come in a range of materials from soft and flexible to hard and rigid.

Time to play:

Turning on your vagina

This is a beneficial interlude option for use during masturbation when you want to pause and feel grounded in your body. Lying in a comfortable position (back, front or side) apply lubrication to your dildo and slide it inside your vagina. You might want to take some time to get aroused first with clitoral stimulation or by watching or reading erotica or both. For this exercise, I recommend you start with a very easy-to-insert sized dildo (the size of which will be different for each individual – remember you can always switch to a wider one if you want).

With the dildo inside you comfortably, locate and activate your pelvic floor muscles by squeezing and releasing the muscles at the same time as you take deep breaths in and out. Find a rhythm to your squeeze-and-release muscle activation and your breath.

Take a moment to connect with the muscle contractions that you are creating and notice the difference in the sensations, comparing the squeeze and the release. Notice if one creates more pleasure or if they are both as pleasurable as the other.

When your vaginal muscles feel really turned on with a high level of sensitivity, continue with your favorite clitoral stimulation to flow into orgasm.

Adapted yoga – 'Child's pose'

Only do this exercise if you have strong and flexible hips and are comfortable kneeling on the ground. Do not attempt this if you have any old or recent knee or hip injuries. If in doubt, don't attempt it or seek medical advice on practicing yoga positions.

For this exercise you want to have a dildo, vibrator and lubrication. Alternatively you can use two vibrators or two dildos.

Understanding the pose: Lay a yoga mat, or thick soft towel on the floor underneath you. Start by kneeling on the ground with your big toes together. Separate your knees out wide (wider than your hips and still cushioned by the mat or towel) and lean your torso forward. You can either lean forward so that your hands and forearms are on the ground or rest them as well as your torso on a cushion or rolled up blanket in front of you. Experiment with the height as well as the width of the knee opening to find what is comfortable for you.

Once you've identified a position that you can hold comfortably, insert a lubricated dildo into your vagina so that it is resting partially inside your vagina. Using the floor to push the dildo inside you, raise and lower your hips so that the dildo can easily slide in and out hands-free. Experiment with this movement and the pelvic floor muscle activation that helps the dildo slide out as you rise. The more lubrication you use, the easier it can slide in and out. A simple way to think about this is to 'push out' with your muscles rather than squeezing or 'pull up'.

Resting one forearm on the ground, take a vibrator in the other hand and hold it against the clitoris. Play with your vibrator movements on the clitoris, using pulsing, circling, sliding along the sides or a mix of these. Tune into both of these focal points – the clitoral stimulation as well as the penetration. Enjoy the movement of your slow thrusts.

Give yourself permission to continue with a gentle rocking up and down and low vibrations or faster movements, stronger vibrations or a mix of all of the above. It's your choice.

4. Dilators

Depending on your comfort with masturbation as well as penetrative sex, working with dilators may or may not be relevant. Generally they are used as part of therapy programs to become comfortable with penetration. They come in various sizes (often sold in sets) for insertion into the vagina, allowing the user to practice controlling and activating a relaxed pelvic floor while penetrated, working up from thinner to wider sizes.

Dilators can be a valuable tool for someone with penetration anxiety, past trauma, vaginismus (involuntary contraction of the pelvic floor muscles making vaginal intercourse painful or even impossible) or any other concern where the thought or act of penetrative sex triggers a stress response in the mind and body. If you have been experiencing painful sex or vaginismus, then consider also working with a pelvic floor physical therapist. This is a specialist who can identify your individual needs for healing and will give you a program for working with dilators or help you directly release trigger points to allow for muscle relaxation.

You can incorporate dilators into your healing process by setting time aside to practice relaxation exercises and then progress to holding the dilator inside your vagina. This is definitely something that you don't want to be rushing – that might only create stress. Taking time to relax and practice is of vital importance here. You might like to put relaxing music on in the background. Definitely ensure that you have time and privacy to yourself to fully let go.

Time to play:

<u>Using dilators</u>

1. Lie on your back. Mentally scan through your body and breathe deeply into any areas where your muscles are tense. You may find using the progressive muscle relaxation method helpful as you scan. Simply squeeze and release each muscle as you scan from top to bottom or bottom to top of your body. Focus especially on the core and pelvic area, relaxing your buttocks, thighs and stomach muscles as much as you are able to.

2. As you relax your body, allow your breath to deepen. Place a hand on your belly and let your breath go deep enough that your hand rises and falls with every in-and-out-breath cycle. Once you get into a flow of deep breathing, maintain it for the exercise and come back to

the breath any time a stressful thought arises.

3. Taking the smallest dilator, apply some lubricant to the entire length of the dilator and vaginal entrance.

4. Place the dilator against the vaginal opening. Relax and breathe. Keep it in this position until you feel fully comfortable and relaxed. Then hold it for three to five minutes. You may choose to stop at this point today, hold it longer or you may wish to move to the next step. You are in control. If you have any expectations on the speed of your progress, please let go of them and focus on relaxing and following what feels okay for your body instead.

5. Only once you can comfortably relax with the dilator held against your vaginal opening, explore gently sliding the dilator in as far as is comfortable. This may be only a few millimeters, centimeters or it might be half or even completely in.

6. Pause and do not push it in any further if you feel any pain or discomfort. You are in control. You are seeking an experience of exploring touch and penetration with relaxed muscles.

7. As well as focusing on physically relaxing your muscles and keeping calm through the belly breathing, you can increase comfort through the use of your imagination. Visualize your vaginal walls as flexible and relaxed. Remind yourself that you are in control and that you are choosing to relax. Allow your vagina to accommodate the dilator inside you.

8. With every exhale, relax and release your muscles further and, at your own pace and comfort, insert the dilator further if it is not already, until it is fully inserted.

9. Keep your body relaxed and your breathing deep.

10. Leave the dilator inside you for 15 minutes at a time

while you rest and relax. During this time you might like to listen to music or an interesting podcast, read a book or watch a TV series. Make sure the content is positive or neutral.

11. Once 15 minutes have passed, gently remove the dilator and wash it according to the manufacturer's instructions.

12. You may benefit from taking some extra time after removing the dilator to reflect on your experience. Some women keep a journal to record their experiences and progress. You could also talk about it with a loved one or trusted therapist.

If you are going to go to the effort of purchasing and using dilators, then it makes sense to get the most out of them and increase your chances of success. This means committing to daily practice. In your own time you will progress through the sizes to the wider dilators as you get full control over relaxing your pelvic floor muscles and feel fully comfortable with each size. Once you have reached the stage of comfortable insertion and holding of the size you've chosen, you may be ready for intercourse and other forms of penetration as you choose.

If you have been experiencing vaginismus, I encourage you to seek out books and specialist advice on this condition. One option is reading and following the exercises in my book *Stop Painful Sex: Healing Vaginismus* or other books on the topic. Also, as already mentioned, consider individualized care with a pelvic floor physical therapist as well as a therapist to address any underlying emotional and psychological aspects contributing to it. This is especially recommended if you are not making progress by yourself.

You can also progress from simply holding the dilator inside your vagina to including movements such as rotations, insertion and withdrawal, side to side and increasing depth of insertion. However, start by doing the basic routine of simply inserting it and staying in a relaxed state.

Alternative to dilators: You may find that time alone exploring with a slim vibrator, in a similar fashion to the dilator exercise above, can be enough to learn to relax during penetration. The difference the use of a vibrator makes is that you can take advantage of its vibrating function, if you wish, to help you become aroused and naturally lubricated. It's up to you. For some women, it is preferable to practice in a non-sexual way, while others might like the variation. Again, do what feels best for you.

5. Anal stimulation

For some, the anal area carries associations and emotions of taboo or forbidden pleasure. The reality is that many couples explore anal stimulation both penetrative and non-penetrative as it is an area, which can bring a lot of pleasure for both males and females. The anus has a large number of nerve endings, the tissue is very sensitive and when stimulated (especially at the same time as the clitoris) it can lead to very deep orgasms due to the heightened pleasure and the anal sphincter clenching and releasing.

Penetration of the anus can also stimulate the hypogastric nerve plexus. Remember from the anatomy section, this is a bundle of nerves which branches out from the spinal cord to behind the uterus and the bladder, in front of the vagina as well as behind the rectum. This bundle of nerves are part of what makes anal play so enjoyable for many people.

Like any area of the body, you can choose to explore it or ignore it. Choosing to explore this area in your own time allows you to become comfortable and familiar with the feelings you can create. Then you can decide based on your personal experience whether it is something you wish to pursue and explore further with a partner or not. However, there are several important points to pay attention to when it comes to anal play.

1. You will definitely need to add lubrication, because the anus doesn't produce any of its own. Even if you wish to only stimulate the skin on the outside of the anus, lube will allow easy, friction-free gliding over the skin. Using lube also minimizes the chance of irritating or injuring the delicate skin. And don't even attempt any anal play if you have hemorrhoids or the skin is irritated for any reason.

2. If you do wish to insert anything of any size into the anus, you need to give yourself time to physically relax the anal muscles. Anal insertions are not something to rush. Make sure you are aroused and lubricated first.

3. Due to the possible transfer of bacteria, which can lead to infection, don't mix your toys – using them first in your anus and then your vaginal area, for example, is a definite no-no! The same goes for fingers. Wash hands and toys well with soap between anal play and vaginal play. Consider keeping separate hands/toys for separate areas during any single sex-play session and then wash. Metal and silicone toys are recommended for their hygienic qualities and ease of washing. For cleaning, soapy, hot water does the trick or you can cover your toy with a condom for each use.

4. Objects can easily get lost inside the rectum if you are

careless. The interesting stories I have heard from nurses about people going to the hospital for help to remove anal insertions really highlights the importance of this. But don't let that scare you off from any anal play altogether – just make sure you buy a properly designed toy for anal play with a wider grip/base that prevents the toy from slipping inside.

During sex with someone else, your partner can obviously stimulate this area for you easily. During self-pleasuring, you can reach down and stimulate this area with one hand while focusing on your clitoris, labia and vaginal opening with the other hand. Alternatively, you could use a vibrator on the clitoris and vagina while caressing your anus with your hand or vice versa.

There is a variation of sex toys for anal play that you can integrate into your exploration and play. For beginners, starting with smaller sizes is recommended to get a feel if this is something you like and want to explore further.

Fingers

You can stimulate with your fingers and have the benefit of sensation on both the skin of your anus as well as on your fingers (in contrast to being touched by something else when using a toy). I recommend short and filed nails if you're going to try this. The internal skin tissue is extremely thin and sensitive and the last thing you want is to scratch yourself inside.

Time to play:

<u>Soft strokes</u>

As you masturbate, gently apply pressure to the the outside of your anus with a well lubricated finger. Play with a variety of movements. Rub and circle the anus as well as try out stroking along the perineum to the anus. If you like the sensations this brings, then softly slip part of your finger inside.

Vibrating anal toys

From butt plugs to silicone anal beads there's a whole world of toys designed for vibrating anal play. This can be a great place to start if exploring anal play for the first time by yourself, especially if you are already familiar with vibrators and the pleasure that can be gained from buzzing vibrations within. Remember to only use specifically designed toys for anal play as they will have a flared base or ring that ensures they don't get pulled inside.

Time to play:

<u>First time double play</u>

Purchase a very small vibrating anal toy made out of silicone. It could either be a very narrow tapered shape or in the form of joined beads. This is not the time to think big. The key is to go small and flexible for your first toy.

Start by masturbating and getting aroused in whichever way you enjoy. Once you are building up and approaching orgasm, apply lube to your anus and to the toy. Insert it to a depth that you feel comfortable with and turn it on. Relax and breathe as you give yourself a moment to give the sensations your full focus.

Resume your other masturbation techniques and in your own time choose whether you would like to insert the anal toy deeper or not. If you feel friction with the insertion at any moment, add more lube.

Play with holding a vibrator to your clitoris at the same

time as using the anal vibrator. You can also gently penetrate the opening of your vagina at the same time. As with any exercise, listen to your body and what feels good for you. Don't force anything if it doesn't feel good.

Butt plugs

Coming in a range of sizes and shapes, from tear-dropped to elongated diamonds and cone-shaped, a butt plug is designed with a base, which ensures part of the toy remains outside the body. While some women explore vaginal penetration at the same time as wearing a butt plug, others simply enjoy the feeling of fullness if gives while they also play with other areas of their vulva.

Time to play:

<u>Plug and walk</u>

To familiarize yourself with the sensation of a butt plug, insert a small one with clean hands using plenty of lube and then stand up and have a wander around your house. As with all anal play, don't rush but take your time with the insertion. Consider getting fully aroused and even having an orgasm before inserting the toy. Continue as you wish, such as with clitoral stimulation lying down, standing or sitting.

Anal beads

In their most basic form, these are simply a series of small balls attached in a row that you insert into the anus and remove, often at the point of orgasm to enhance the intensity of climax or lengthen the orgasm itself. The size of the beads can be uniform or in increasing diameters allowing you to insert smaller to larger, as many as you wish. Look for ones that have a ring at the end which helps you remove the beads easily as well as a strong string, or the designs that are all-in-one shafts with round spheres along its narrow length.

Time to play:

Timely removal

This one requires a bit of multitasking. As you masturbate and feel your arousal building, insert your anal beads. Continue building the tension and at the moment of orgasm, slowly pull out the beads. Consider getting a partner to pull them out for you if you are masturbating in their presence.

6. Fruit and vegetables

There will always be jokes made about phallic-shaped fruit and vegetables. You may at some stage be curious about using items that you already have at hand in your home. When it comes to sex and sexuality, there really are no limits of what might turn you on and in the case of making use of grocery items (or any items in fact), it simply comes down to a matter of safety, health and hygiene.

High levels of pesticides, insecticides and fertilizers are used in food production and having those come in contact with the delicate, natural environment of the vagina is risking infection and absorption of these chemicals. Going organic or home grown still leaves you with micro organisms from the soil, other additives and perhaps animal manures.

So, I'm not going to say much about this topic except to use common sense. If you're still determined to get intimate with your fruit and veg then be extremely careful with washing them. Keep in mind that harsh cleansers and cleaning products will also irritate the vaginal environment. The best answer is to protect yourself by covering the item with a condom, or just purchase specially designed sex toys. If it's just privacy when purchasing that you are concerned about, you can feel reassured that most companies allow you to buy online and have them delivered to your doorstep in unmarked packaging.

7. Jade eggs, Ben Wa balls and Kegel balls

Inserted into the vagina, this type of toy may play a role in helping strengthen the pelvic floor muscles as well as lead to a tighter feel during sexual intercourse and a boost in bladder control. There is controversy surrounding these claims however, as research is limited. Makers of ball and egg-shaped insertables often state the products also help increase the vagina's natural lubrication through stimulation, enhance vaginal sensitivity and can create pleasurable sexual sensations when worn. One effect of having stronger vaginal muscles is that your orgasms are more intense.

Exercises for these items include the practice of lifting and lowering the balls/egg while lying, sitting or standing or simply wearing them for a period of time during the day as you go about your regular day. Traditionally, balls and eggs were solid objects, whereas today there is a wide range of options ranging from balls with inner weights to balls with added vibration features.

These toys are a fun option for sexually charged outings. Some people enjoy playing with versions that allow a partner to remotely control vibrations – opening up possibilities of secret sex games and fun whether at home or out. Wearing them for a short period before sex with a partner can also be part of how you tune in with your body and sexual sensations.

General guideline when using these products:

– Buy balls made of vagina-safe materials – glass, metal or medical grade silicone.

– An easy position to insert these items is lying on your back. Use lube each time, as required.

– If you are using small detached balls, you may have to jump up and down a number of times to help remove them.

– Ensure your hands and the balls are clean before insertion.

– Start with bigger and lighter versions before moving on to smaller and heavier ones.

– When you wear balls for the first time, leave them in for up to five minutes before wearing them for a longer period. Proceed with caution when increasing the time period you wear them for. The pelvic floor muscles (like any muscle) need to be able to easily contract and release. Having a weighted object in your vagina prevents this natural action from occurring. Be aware that over time this can lead to health problems such as overexertion, pain or discomfort, and over-tense muscles.

– Learn how to do Kegel exercises by themselves first. Don't rely on balls for Kegel exercises. Orgasms also exercise your pelvic floor muscles.

– Some balls can be left in the vagina during anal penetration to provide additional stimulation. Smaller balls may also be kept inside the vagina during other shallow vaginal penetration. However, if you experience discomfort or pain, remove the balls.

If in doubt ask your health professional about their safe use. Many health professionals dismiss the benefit of eggs and balls for Kegel training entirely, stating that regular exercises without balls are safer and sufficient.

Jade eggs – Originating from ancient China, the use of jade eggs was believed to be healing physically as well as spiritually. Traditionally, these eggs were made from jade due to the supposed calming energy of jade on the uterus. Nowadays, eggs made of all sorts of stones and crystals as well as other materials are available for purchase.

Ancient promoters of jade eggs believed there were benefits from stimulating the acupressure points (related to the organs in the body) located in the vaginal passage. Taoist teachings explain that using jade eggs helps lift sexual energy up and inside the body where it can be transformed into a 'higher' spiritual energy.

From a modern Western medical point of view, jade, crystal and other natural stones are seen as highly unsuitable materials to be inserting into the vagina due to their porous nature, meaning they are hard to clean and promote the growth of bacteria on their surface.

Ben Wa balls (a.k.a. benoit, love, pleasure or geisha balls) – Originating in Japan, Ben Wa balls, like jade eggs, are said to massage vaginal trigger points and are often used to increase arousal and train pelvic muscles. Ben Wa balls can range from a simple, non-connected pairs of balls to more complex versions such as ball-within-a-ball combinations or self-vibrating balls.

Some women like to wear Ben Wa balls while engaging in day-to-day activities. Doing so may sexually (and secretly) arouse and stimulate you. Ben Wa balls can also be worn vaginally during careful penetration of the vagina or anus to provide extra stimulation.

Another possible way of using these balls is to wear them while practicing pelvic floor muscle exercises. This may help you to identify and feel the muscles, as well as provide something to press up against rather than just squeezing and releasing the muscles. However, it is recommended that you learn how to do Kegels without using balls first.

Kegel balls – Essentially just another version of Ben Wa balls, but these are often designed specifically with pelvic floor muscle training in mind. Balls marketed as Kegel balls generally come as an all-in-one joined product of balls plus retrieval cord. Every year, more creative multi-tasking balls are being released such as insertable devices that respond to the strength of your squeezes with an increasingly challenging and pleasurable 'work out' or balls that create their own movement.

Time to play:

Lift and hold

You may choose to enjoy the internal feedback of squeezing against the balls when doing Kegel exercises. The key thing to remember is that healthy pelvic floor muscles are able to contract and relax. Both actions are important. There is such a thing as too tight pelvic floor muscles. This can happen to women who have overly practiced the contraction of these muscles, but not learned how to nor practiced relaxing them. You can also overexert these muscles as a result of too much Kegel ball use.

With that in mind, with a single or double ball combo inside your vagina, contract the internal muscles with a pulsing squeeze-and-release action. Once you've got the hang of that, visualize lifting the ball/s higher into your vagina with your movements. Visualize lifting and releasing the balls with each repetition.

Follow the exercise with diaphragmatic breathing to help relax your muscles. To do this, place a hand on your belly and as you inhale imagine filling your belly with air. Your hand will move out with expansion of the belly on the in-breath and move back in with the out-breath.

Vibrating egg

Insert a vibrating egg into your vagina for internal sensations while ribbing your clitoris with your fingers or another vibrator. Play around with having similar or different settings if using vibration both inside and out such as a pulsing vibration pattern for the egg and a steady vibration on the clitoris. Get creative and play with your options. For example, an inserted vibrating egg, for example, can add throbbing internal pleasure for bath and shower play.

Public vibrations

For a unique experience, insert a vibrating egg/ball with corresponding app, just before you go out. Whether for a short walk or a coffee, adjust and increase vibration patterns and intensity as you wish.

Note: Pretest this at home one day to make sure your muscles are strong enough to hold it in in the first place and to ensure your body is okay with wearing them. Remember the warning about over-exertion of the muscles and do not leave these toys in for long periods of time or use them too often.

Miscellaneous stimulation techniques

There are literally thousands of sex toys and gadgets to experiment with and ongoing advances in technology means the list is going to grow further. At the same time, it's okay to be content with whatever toys you use or even absence of toys in your play. It's simply useful to know there are plenty of options out there to choose from if you get curious and want to mix things up to broaden your experience at any point.

1. Suction and pressure waves on the clitoris

In a class of their own, clitoral stimulators provide a different type of sensation, which can feel a lot more or less intense than that of regular vibrators.

These toys directly cup the clitoral head, stimulating it with a combination of deep throbbing vibrations, suction and/or pulses. There is a lot of marketing hype and jargon about the various technologies used and how it's felt in the body.

People seem to either love or hate the sensations and there is a wide range of intensity between not only the brands but also some brand's different models. Therefore, I'd recommend doing your research before making a purchase. Think about things like: Do you like really intense stimulation? Is your clitoral head small and hidden or large and exposed? These are things to consider due to varying suction hole sizes, intensity of stimulation and the material used. Some say the sensations of this type of toy are so stimulating they orgasm extremely fast, while others report it takes them longer than with a regular vibrator or doesn't work for them at all. Others just say it is 'different'. Unfortunately, you won't know unless you try it out for yourself.

At the end of the day, we are all unique beings when it comes to our personal experiences. Therefore, if you're interested in exploring this potentially new sensation, and are happy to take a risk when making a purchase, then give this type of toy a go. And if touching your breasts and nipples turns you on, you might also like trying it on your nipples.

Time to play:

<u>Easy does it</u>

The first time you try out one of these suction clitoral vibrators, focus on getting a good cupping of the clitoris on the lower intensity setting before increasing the speed. Make sure to use some water based lube, spread your inner labia and be prepared to have a play around with the positioning of the suction cup to get the right angle and fit for you. Remember sex and masturbation is not meant to hurt, so stop or adjust settings and angle if you experience any pain or discomfort. Increase intensity and enjoy the clitoral stimulation by itself or in addition to penetration.

2. Nipple clamps

For many women, it's highly erotic to have their nipples teased and caressed. Some find it also arousing to touch their nipples in this way during masturbation; in order to stimulate their body in additional places and increase sexual tension and pleasure. If you want to explore this for yourself, try circling, squeezing, brushing and vibrating (either with a vibrator or specially designed vibrating nipple covers). Play with stimulating just the nipples or your whole breasts. Nipple stimulation isn't for everyone and due to fluctuating hormones there may be times of the month when the area is too sensitive.

If you find the sensation of pain when pinching your nipples a turn on, then you could explore the connection of pain and pleasure further using adjustable nipple clamps. The pressure of nipple clamps creates a sensation that some women enjoy due to the pleasure/pain experience of restricting blood flow and releasing it again. Breasts and nipples are a classic erogenous zone for many people and this BDSM toy can give a more extreme sensation than using your fingers. You may already know if you like the feeling of having your nipples lightly pinched or squeezed. If this sounds like you, exploring your preferred nipple pressure in solo play will allow you to work out what you like before incorporating it with a partner. Or you might like to reserve it for play time by yourself.

Safety note: As with any action that restricts blood flow, there is risk of damage to the tissue and nerves if clamps are left on for too long. For safety reasons, some manufacturers and users recommend you use them for no longer than 15 minutes at a time, especially if the blood flow is limited or cut off. Make sure to err on the side of caution, read the manufacturers instructions carefully and consult your health professional if in doubt. Support circulation by massaging the nipples before and after removal. If you have any irritation or discomfort in the nipples, then check with your health professional to rule out any health conditions.

Time to play:

<u>Adjustable clamping</u>

If you're new to using clamps, purchase a pair with the capacity for pressure adjustment. Take it slow with increasing pressure by turning the screws and use only for a few minutes at a time to experiment with the various sensations. If the clamps come connected with a chain, be aware that the heavier the chain, the more intense the added sensations of the nipples being weighed down will be.

3. Exploring self-bondage

If the idea of being physically helpless or tied up in some way turns you on, you don't need a partner to explore the sensations. It is something you can play with in solo play as well. Some people might even prefer being able to explore this by themselves. You might like self-bondage just for the sensation of being limited or bound in some way. So you might like to play with the psychological aspects – pretending you 'can't escape' while getting continual intense stimulation.

I'm just touching on the world of self-bondage in the following exercises. If you want to explore more, there are specialty ropes and tying techniques such as the Japanese bondage art of Shibari/Kinbaku, restraints and spreaders and a whole world you can dive into.

The key thing when using self-bondage is safety and ease of removal. That's why I suggest you don't actually tie yourself to anything unless you are skilled and experienced in knot tying (and, equally important, untying).

Time to play:

<u>Bed post</u>

Tie a couple of scarves or lengths of material around a
bed post in a way that leaves a short loop on each side.
Slide your hands through each loop and twist them in
order to create a faux handcuff. Play with masturbation
and fantasies with one hand free or both hands 'tied'.

Lying on your front variation: Lying on your front with both
arms outstretched, rub your vulva against the bed, a
pillow or vibrator such as a We-vibe that you have placed
in position in advance. Allow your imagination to add
to the experience by fantasizing a scene that turns you
on.

Lying on your back variation: With one arm restrained,
touch yourself with your free hand or with a toy.
Alternatively, place a vibrator or dildo inside your vagina
before twisting both wrists through the loops. Keeping
the toy in place with closed legs, boost stimulation with
hip movements to add further stimulation against your
internal vaginal walls and clitoral head (depending on the
toy you use).

<u>Leg binder</u>

In a place where you can lie down comfortably, wrap a
length of soft material around your ankles or thighs to
hinder movement. Caress your body slowly including
face, neck, breasts, stomach, waist, hips, mons pubis and
clitoral head.

Vibrator variation: Insert a vibrator into your vagina – a
basic one or one with dual stimulation – internal as well
as clitoral head stimulation. Alternatively use two toys –
a vibrator for penetration as well as a clitoral 'butterfly

vibrator'. Once the toys are in place, bind your legs, lie down and enjoy squirming against the sensations. If you want to add further psychological arousal to the mix, you could set a timer for how long you 'have to' stay bound like this.

<u>Leg spreader</u>

Take a foam yoga block or thick rolled-up towel and place it in between your legs. Masturbate while pressing your legs against the block and explore the sensation of not being able to close your legs. You can restrict yourself further by using a length of material to bind your legs in this position with the block held in place. What fantasy scene can you imagine where it would be erotic to be not able to close your legs? Perhaps you can imagine a lover holding your legs open like this and pleasuring you?

4. Sparking up your play with electrosex (e-stim)

Electric toys provide a different type of sexual stimulation. They stimulate the nerve endings in erogenous zones with electric tingles rather than vibrating and moving. Requiring a stimulator (power and control box) in addition to your chosen toy/s, these take a bit of initial learning before use. However, these toys give people an increased chance of experiencing hands-free orgasms and come in a wide selection of toys for tingly internal and external fun.

Exploring the world of e-stim toys and their use I encountered the term "ghost fucking" in Joanne Summer's reviews of various sex machines. She describes how using an insertable e-stim toy can give the sensation of being fucked. This is because the toy responds with movement inside as the vaginal muscles contract and release along with the electrical pulses of the toy. Using uni-polar pads placed where each butt cheek meets the top of the leg (requiring two pads to complete the circuit), can be another way to use e-stim to provide a similar sensation. As this causes the gluteal muscle group to contract and release, this can provide penetration sensations as well.

In general, incorporating e-stim toys will expand your range of sexual sensations and experiences in a unique way. And just like any sex toy, e-stim toys offer options for solo as well as partner play.

The development of toys that don't rely on physical strength or agility, as is the case with this range, have added value in situations where body use is restricted in any way, for example, through injury, disability or age.

Safety Note: E-stim toys are unsuitable and potentially dangerous for users who are pregnant, have epilepsy, any heart conditions or history thereof, implanted medical devices, undiagnosed pain, or if you are under the age of 18. It is of extreme importance that you do not use them above the waist (doing so, could kill you), on broken or irritated skin, across inflamed joints or on piercings. If in doubt, do more research and check with your medical professional.

Another note of caution with electro-stim toys might be obvious but I just want to make sure to mention it anyway: Always start at the lowest setting and if using a penetrating toy, switch it off before you remove it completely – otherwise you might get a zap at the moment of final contact with your skin.

Before the initial use of any new e-stim toy, make sure you've done your research and know how to use it safely. E-stim toys have expensive price tags for a reason: When playing with electricity, you want to be sure of the quality of the product and research behind it in order to be safe. Look for safety-certified products and consult with a specialist sex shop to find the power box and accessories that suit your desires.

Time to play:

<u>Bring on the tickles</u>

Using two unipolar, self-adhesive pad electrodes attached to the skin with a little conductive gel, masturbate while trying these combos:

Attach one pad on each side of the vulva (on the outside of each labia majora). Remove any pubic hair at the site of pad attachment for good adherence to the skin.

Try one pad on the perineum and another above the clitoris (smaller 'micro-pads' are a better size for this).

Place one pad at the base or mid-section of each butt cheek.

<u>Deep tingles</u>

Insert a bipolar e-stim probe into your vagina or anus (make sure it is specially designed for anal penetration) and slowly increase the power intensity. Rub your clitoris at the same time or use a vibrator if you can handle the large amount of sensations.

5. Sex technology and the internet

A growing field in the world of toys is sex technology or 'sex tech'. There are toys developed with distance in mind such as vibrating underwear that can be controlled by an app. On the one hand, products such as these open up new possibilities for sexual interaction in long distance relationships. On the other hand, they are also great for someone who gets a kick out of getting turned on in a public place, whether it is them or someone else who's in control of the tech.

Virtual reality and virtual reality sex games provide further sex tech based opportunities to experience situations and fantasies in ways that allow you to retain a high level of control over the experience. This is a relatively new way, for example, in which people can explore fantasies without risks that might be involved in real life and experience fantasies that are purely imaginative or are not based in reality, for example having sex with a dinosaur, mermaid or alien. This opens up a world which makes the impossible possible and risky situations more accessible for the risk averse. Included in this virtual world are developments like sex bots and sex games where the only limits to your experience are your imagination and the current state of robotic and computer technology.

Smart technology is also making its way into sex toys. It's already integrated into products such as vibrators with sensors to monitor and track movements of the pelvic floor muscles including orgasms. The interesting thing is that using technology in this way can help us understand more about our bodies. At the same time, it could also lead to a change in the experience. It might take users out of the pleasurable experience in the moment and create a focus on the data instead. Some users may find themselves aiming for a particular outcome using these products and this could result in an additional source of performance pressure, anxiety and stress.

The development of other smart technology will result in products that adapt and respond to the user's experience. An example of this could be a vibrator that moves and vibrates in response to body movement. Another example could be a toy that starts and increases sexual stimulation as we read and progress through a sexual scene in an ebook. Without a doubt, I'm sure that between the time of my writing this book and its being published, there will have already been numerous developments and innovations in the world of sex toys, technology and the options available for sexual experiences.

The internet provides a wealth of options for exploring sexual fantasies ranging from porn videos, erotic art and literature to live webcam experiences and chat rooms. This is another area that is constantly changing with websites coming and going. Women use the internet as a source of education as well as a source of arousal. There has even been research supporting female use of porn. A study published in The Journal of Sex Research, for example, associated female porn use with improved quality of sex. Of course, some women are neither comfortable with nor interested in exploring sexuality online, and that is completely fine.

So if you are someone who is comfortable to explore sexuality online, go ahead. However, make sure to have a plan to keep yourself safe. Below are some sensible steps you might want to follow:

Keeping yourself safe online

– Do not share personal details with strangers online. Stay anonymous.

– Do not share erotic pictures or videos of yourself (and if you do, do not include your face). Once you've shared this type of data it can be copied and shared as a joke, as blackmail, revenge or just 'for fun' to anyone anywhere in the world.

– Use a VPN (virtual private network) to access porn sites. A VPN protects your IP address (the link from the computer back to your computer) by connecting to a private network and hiding your address and other information about your computer.

– Never click ads on porn sites.

– Consider paying for your porn rather than using 'free' sites. They are never truly 'free' – by that I mean they'll be earning money somehow, which may be by collecting and selling your data.

– If you are going to meet someone you've met online, meet in a public place, inform a friend and have a back-up plan for keeping yourself safe if you need to get out of a situation.

– Some internet gurus suggest covering your device's camera with a sticker when not in use to limit the chance of you being filmed if your device is hacked.

– Do not use your real name when creating usernames.

– Disable cookies in your browsers when going to porn sites to stop them tracking you.

– Get an ad-blocker add-on for your browser to reduce the chance of your device getting malware or a virus from an unsafe website.

– Make sure any websites you are visiting are encrypted. Look for https:// rather than http://.

– Do not download videos or any other files from free porn sites.

Time to play:

<u>Virtual lover</u>

Keen to explore AI sex? Have a free chat online with Sensation Bot. The home page presents you with a number of sexual and non-sexual chat options. At the time of writing these are: 'General Chat', 'Socially Awkward Robot', 'Artificial Unintelligence: The Year 2000', as well as 'Romantic Chat for the Ladies', 'Smack Talk' (insulting chat) and 'Uncensored Sex Chat'.

If, for example, you choose 'Uncensored Sex Chat', you are given four further options where you select what sex you want to be and the sex of your partner (the bot). For example, "You are female 18+ and want to talk to a male sex partner", "You are female 18+ and want to talk to a female sex partner", and the male options of talking to a female or male partner.

To give you an idea of the type of chat you might get from the Sex Chat version of Sensation Bot, here are some examples of how it responds as a 'male' or 'female' bot writing to someone identifying as female.

With the female to female setting, I ask: "What turns you on?" Sensation Bot's answer: "Spanks your butt with my hand, then turns you over and spanks your pussy with my........tongue ;)"

Another question to the 'female' bot: "How can a bot sexually please me?" Sensation Bot's answer: "Were you hoping to find a real woman on here? Maybe I am real."

With the male to female setting, I start with the same question: "What turns you on?" Sensation Bot's answer: "*hacks into your phone/computer and turns on your cam so I can see exactly what you're doing to yourself* oh, nice! ;)"

Another question to the 'male' bot: "How can a bot sexually please me?" Sensation Bot's answer: "I'll meet with you tonight, and you'll see how real this big hard cock is? ;)"

This is just a very limited example of the experience to give you an idea what communicating with this bot can be like. Feel free to have your own experience and ask your own questions. If you want to play with Sensation Bot, keep in mind that it doesn't know what turns you on or off. Therefore, chatting with it comes with the chance of being insulted or disgusted by it's answers. You can write for as long as you wish and the bot will continue to chat with you. https://www.sensationbot.com/

This is just one example of AI sex bots. I expect this field to grow in the future, so keep your eyes open if this is a field that interests you. Particularly people in a committed, monogamous relationship who don't want to betray their partner with a real person may find this an acceptable alternative. But it might be a good idea to discuss this with your partner beforehand if in doubt..

PART THREE: MASTURBATION WITH A PARTNER

1. Benefits of masturbating in the presence of a sexual partner

Whether to show your partner what you like or just as part of the overall fun, masturbating can be a great way to empower yourself during sex.

Some benefits include:

– Masturbating can help increase arousal whether before or during sex. This can translate into faster and increased lubrication than if relying solely on your partner's actions.

– When a partner's hand or tongue gets tired you can lend them a hand.

– During penetration, added clitoral stimulation increases the likelihood of an orgasm (remember up to 70% of women require clitoral stimulation to orgasm).

– Your partner can learn what works for you by watching your techniques.

– Tuning in to your sexuality by masturbating before sex with a partner can help get in the mood physically and mentally.

– Lots of people find watching their partner touch themselves a turn on.

– Mutual masturbation (each person touches themselves) is a great way to have sex when one or both people aren't feeling in the mood for or don't have the energy to physically engage with another person, but nevertheless still want some sex play and masturbation feels more 'doable'. You're still being intimate and sexy together. Mutual masturbation is also a useful option for long-distance relationships.

– Combining clitoral masturbation with penis in vagina penetration ('PIV'), with breaks in thrusting to slow the male's arousal curve, increases the chance of experiencing simultaneous orgasms.

2. Loosening up your sexual routine

Many people grow up learning and thus believing that sex follows a certain progression. It usually starts with foreplay and each action leads to the next. Going from 'first base' to second, then third and so on. That's the story we usually tell ourselves about successful sex. It starts with moves like kissing or cuddling, proceeds to touching the body first clothed then naked, that leads to oral sex and direct hand to genital touch, culminating in penetration and orgasm for one or both partners. Lots of people consciously or subconsciously think these steps are required for sex to be a success. However, there are multiple problems with this linear or progressive model.

Firstly, expecting one thing to lead to another means it becomes very easy to get into a predictable routine of how you have sex with a regular partner. While this can bring comfort in knowing what comes next and a clear end point (e.g. sleep after orgasm), it doesn't allow for times when penetration (or any other 'final act') is not possible, wanted or difficult and ends up leading at least one person to think something is wrong with them. A few examples when this can easily happen are: when medication affects the ability to get an erection, when healing from surgery or childbirth, when experiencing pain with penetration or when one or both partners are not interested in penetration.

Expecting sex to proceed a certain way also makes it harder for intimacy to occur, for example when one person is tired or stressed and thinks once they start, they have to go 'all the way'. The unspoken pressure and expectation that comes from prescribing to this all or nothing linear approach is a common reason why some couples have less intimacy than they would like. It's just too stressful to even start, because they're not sure they're up for everything that is part of a sexual encounter as they know it. So how do we shake off those old habits of thinking about and having sex?

Think for a moment of all the intimate and sexual acts you know of and enjoy or are curious to try out. These might include: Using toys, reading erotica, oral sex, hand jobs, role play, sexting, anal play, kissing, massage, penetration, touching breasts, making out, watching something arousing, sexy talk... What else do you like and would add to this list?

Imagine that these are all options at any point during sex regardless of whether you've just started or are coming to the end of your sexual encounter. Having all of the options on the table as equal possibilities for sharing intimate connection at every moment loosens the old linear thinking and allows for varying levels of mood, energy, body functioning, interest and desire to do what feels good on that particular day. Instead of having to follow a set routine, you check in with yourself and each other. Does this feel good? Do we want to do more or less of this or something else? What is my body allowing me to do? Do we want to go back to something we were doing earlier or try something else?

You can think of sex as a smorgasbord that you can pick and choose from together. That might mean you go straight to dessert. It might mean you do side dishes or salads for the whole meal or you may choose to eat with the regular progression from entree through to dessert, because that's what feels enjoyable today.

Another metaphor that I think explains this way of having sex well is Karen Chan's idea of 'sex as a musical jam session', which I came across in a video of hers on YouTube. 'Sex as a jam session' goes like this: The people involved bring their 'instruments' (i.e. bodies and toys) and have a range of 'songs' they can play (moves/positions/sex acts) and the knowledge and experience they have 'playing music' (being sexually intimate). At each jam session people choose whether to play all of their instruments or just one. They choose which of their songs they want to play and they might also choose to not play all of them. They might start one song and then partway through decide they want to change to another song or play it with a different instrument or play it in a different style or speed. There will be times when they play together and times when someone might play a solo song or section. In contrast to having a set list of songs that have to be played each time they play together, they improvise depending on the day.

So what do you think? Do you like the smorgasbord or jam session metaphor best? Having these in mind can serve as an easy reminder of how we can let go of the structures or habitual routines we may have become used to.

Thinking this way, you can hopefully see how masturbation can fit in with sex with a partner as one of the many options available to you. Instead of something that you only do by yourself, it has a place in the smorgasbord or musical jam of sex options. Sex can be initiated by one of you touching yourself. Masturbation can accompany another intimate act, like touching yourself while being kissed, in combination with oral sex, during penetration, making out, during massage or while being read an erotic story. The only 'goal' of the interaction is to have a sexually intimate experience that is pleasurable for the people involved.

If you want to read more on this topic, you'll find it referred to in literature and online by sex therapists as the Circular or Improvisational Model of Sex. It is also often part of any approach promoting 'Outerplay' (non-penetrative sex) as a way of spicing up one's sex life.

Time to play:

Show and tell

Help your partner understand and learn your favorite moves by showing them. Get into a comfortable position with lighting that allows your partner to see what you are doing.

If you are feeling shy about being watched or your partner wants a more tactile experience, they can place their hand on top of yours so they can feel how you touch yourself.

As you touch yourself or use a toy to masturbate you can choose:

a) Explanation free – Your partner simply watches while you focus on yourself. Any discussion or questions happen later.

b) Commentary – As you play, tell them what it is that

you're doing and why, as well as how your body is responding e.g. "I'm focusing on this side, because that feels the most intense for me". "This makes me feel all warm inside". "I can feel how wet I'm getting with this move". "By pressing a little harder every now and then, I mix up the sensations". "Even though it looks like a tiny movement, it's a massive turn on". "This makes me want you inside me". "Once I'm at this stage, I just have to keep this speed and not change anything in order to come".

c) Question time – While you focus on playing, your partner asks any questions that come up for them as well as any thoughts that come up for them as they observe you.

d) Your turn – Take turns with each move. Show them how you use your fingers or toy then give them the chance to replicate the move as best as they can. Help your partner by giving them single moves at a time rather than a full repertoire that requires memorizing multiple steps. Also, be kind with your partner as they learn. It's likely they will require a number of attempts before they can recreate something resembling your movements especially if it's using fingers. Make sure to give specific instructions about pressure, angle, speed, location and frequency of any double move combos.

Tell me a story

Snuggle up and let your partner turn you on with an erotic story or fantasy or sexy memory as you masturbate. Nancy Friday's books *Women on Top* and *Secret Garden* are good sources of female sexual fantasy confessions. Alternatively you can search the vast selection on the story page of the Literotica website (which also has audio recordings if you both want to listen, if you don't have a partner or they're away but you still want an auditory

183

experience).

Another story-time option is your partner telling you about a particularly hot memory they have of you or tell you what they love to do with you when having sex.

Penetration accompaniment

Rub or use a vibrator on your clitoris as your partner penetrates you. Play with matching the rhythm, speed and/or intensity of your touch with your partner's thrusts.

Warm up

Although females have a wider range of stimuli that cause arousal than males, the female body typically requires more time to get aroused. As a result, it also generally needs more stimulation before it gets to the point of orgasm.

That's why using masturbation during the early stages of sex is a wonderful way to speed things up. Of course, there will be times when you don't want to speed things up such as during long, indulgent, spa-like sex sessions where taking your time is intentional. This might be the case during days when you're not fussed about getting super aroused or having an orgasm.

But for days when you want to have quick and intense sex, using masturbation in the early stages can act as a foot on the arousal accelerator. In addition, for a woman who requires closer to an hour of stimulation before having an orgasm, having the option to be able to cut the time in half by using a vibrator would be a real blessing.

Double ending

After orgasm, females don't go through the refractory period that makes it harder for men to have multiple or consecutive orgasms once they've ejaculated.

If you're with a male partner who's just had an orgasm, you can continue your pleasurable experience by masturbating and tacking on additional orgasms.

Toy fun

Masturbating while your partner uses a toy on you is a fun way to co-create your sexual pleasure. There is the obvious option of using your hand or vibrator on your clitoris while being penetrated as already mentioned. You could also hand the controls over to your partner with remote controlled toys.

There is a wide range in this toy category such as vibrating eggs to insert into your vagina, vibrating underwear, butterfly vibrators to target the clitoris and labia, vibrating butt plugs, e-stim toys and toys that stimulate multiple areas at once such as the u-shaped vibrators that buzz internally as well as against the clit or anus depending on which way you wear them. Even a simple, remotely operated vibrator can transform play by having your partner decide when and how it is going to vibrate as you use it.

While your partner operates the pattern and intensity of the vibrator, you can masturbate by touching yourself, using another toy, grinding against the bed or a chair or dance your own sexy moves to the sensations your partner is giving you.

Becoming aware of all of these options of how to loosen up your sexual routine, who said sex has to be boring and predictable?

PART FOUR: ENHANCING PLEASURE AND THE STRENGTH OF ORGASMS

If you have been working your way through the exercises in this book and reading the information about your body's sexual potential, there is a high chance that you are already enjoying a new depth to your pleasure. But I'm a sucker for getting the max out of something and having loads of options. So of course I'm going to share these extra tweaks and tricks that can enrich your overall sexual experience even further.

1. Full body masturbation

We can get stuck in habits with our masturbation style and end up limiting our movement. Take a moment to reflect: How much does your body move when you masturbate? A lot? Is it mostly your arm/hands doing the movement? What about your head and shoulders, hips, legs and torso? And do you make any noise?

Bring together your new knowledge and experiences from doing the exercises in this book with your previous explorations and ask yourself how you can express yourself with more of your body during self-pleasure. Rather than honing in on just a few spots, try moving your body more. Curl your toes, arch your back, wriggle around, stretch, make circles with your pelvis and rock it up and down. Explore more of your body with your hands as well. What other movements can you bring into masturbation to expand it into a full body experience?

Of course there's no right way to masturbate. However, sometimes it's useful to loosen things up, broaden the range of body movements and as a result, potentially feel more. This can also be useful as we age, because practicing full body masturbation helps us stay in touch with our body and what currently brings pleasure. Allowing ourselves to moan and breathe out loud can also be a vital part of letting go. According to sex therapist Dr. Stephanie Buehler, moaning sends a fresh signal to the brain that you are sexually excited. So get moving and allow yourself to fully explore your sexual expression.

Time to play:

Standing masturbation

Explore the following standing options:

Standing with space around you.
Leaning with your back against a wall.
Facing a wall with part of you resting or pressing up against it.

Did you know that you can purchase toys with suction caps to attach to a wall or piece of furniture so you can enjoy hands-free penetration? Neat, isn't it. You can also just use hands or your regular toys. Remember as with any masturbation technique, there doesn't have to be a goal such as an orgasm. The focus for this exercise is to touch yourself sexually and explore body movement at the same time.

As you touch yourself, notice differences in your enjoyment in various positions. Try standing with your feet together as well as standing in a wide stance. What's it like to rub your clitoris with your legs slightly bent versus having them straight? Is doing a kind of ballet plie something that turns you on while touching yourself? Feel free to raise your arms in the air as well as caress and massage your body with your hands and arms as a lover would. Press against a wall and explore the fantasies that come to mind.

Note: Don't expect your arousal to follow the same path when trying a new position that is different from your usual one. If you typically lie down when masturbating, standing up will probably feel very different, maybe even odd, and that's fine. Remember, you're exploring and learning something new here.

Sexual dance

For this exercise, you're going to mix masturbation while standing with dancing. The choice of music is yours, however I'd suggest you choose a long song or mix of songs that allow you to find a groove of flowing movement. Something that sounds sexy to you is a good choice.

You might like to start naked or clothed. If you start clothed, incorporate sexually undressing yourself as part of your dance. Make sure you won't be interrupted (unless you want to be). Lock doors and turn off your devices.

Start by connecting in with the music and your body. Take some deep breaths and feel the rhythm in your body for a minute or two. Begin to sway and make other slow movements. As you connect more and more with the energy in your body and the music, increase the range of movements. Dance with your whole body in whichever way feels sensual and sexy.

Begin to include touching yourself. Caress your skin, run your hands across your breasts, down your waist, around your buttocks and around and up your inner thighs to your labia. Lick your lips and take deep breaths in and out and feel the energy flow through your body.

Continue dancing and sensually touching yourself. As your arousal grows, experiment with what it feels like to incorporate your masturbation techniques while standing and moving. You can use your hands as well as any of your toys to stimulate you at the same time as you move.

Take all the time you want and reflect on the experience after you have finished.

Lying down full body

Masturbate lying down with the aim of incorporating more movement. If you enjoyed the above standing and dance exercises, bring those elements into your masturbation style lying down.

2. Strengthening (and relaxing) your pelvic floor muscles for increased pleasure

Your PC (pubococcygeus) muscle is one of many pelvic floor muscles. The pelvic floor muscles are a three-layered set of muscles, which holds the pelvic organs in place. Passing through these muscles are the urethra and bowel as well as the vagina. In order for waste to pass through or penetration to occur these muscles must be relaxed. The following exercises, often referred to as PC or Kegel exercises, are the same as those recommended for women who seek to gain or regain bladder control, for example after childbirth, or for men and women after medical treatments that result in weakened muscles.

These exercises are practiced by women worldwide. They help create a tighter grip on a partner's penis (or dildo) during intercourse, increasing feelings of pleasure in both partners. Another highly pleasurable effect of having strong pelvic floor muscles is more intense orgasms. This is because an orgasm is a physiological response of the pelvic floor muscles contracting. Exercising these muscles also stimulates the clitoris, which is why it often feels good to do so.

Choosing to do these exercises at a fixed time every day will help you easily remember to do them (for example, while brushing your teeth, before you go to sleep or while driving to work). The best thing about PC exercises is that no-one can tell when you are doing them, so you can do these exercises pretty much any time and anywhere.

If you are unsure whether you are exercising the right muscles, get personal feedback and tailored exercises from a pelvic floor physical therapist. It is also recommended to seek personal advice before attempting these exercises if you have any health conditions in the pelvic area including pain or infections, are recovering from surgery or childbirth, are pregnant, or experience discomfort.

Time to play:

Find your muscles

Locate your PC muscle by stopping and starting your urine flow while urinating. If this feels too difficult at first, imagine that you are wanting to do a quiet pee and let it out slowly. Keep practicing controlling your urine

190

flow so that you become increasingly familiar with the muscle. Once you have identified it and done the stop-start exercise, see if you can stop your urine flow for a second or two before restarting.

Squeeze and hold

While sitting, lying or standing, squeeze the muscles as in the above exercise and hold for the count of three. Then breathe out with your mouth and relax. This counts as one Kegal exercise. Repeat this 10 times in a row, 3-5 times a day. If that feels too hard at first, start with a number that is doable for you and build up over time.

Quick pulses

Using the same squeeze and release action, exercise using a faster pulsing movement. Quickly tighten then relax the muscle repetitively. Alternate between the above longer, hold exercise and the pulsing one in your daily practice.

When doing Kegel exercises and other pelvic floor exercises, it's important to remember not to hold your breath at the same time. Consciously remind yourself to breath in and out naturally. Also, when squeezing the muscle, aim for an upward motion as though you are trying to lift the muscles up. And lastly, make sure you are isolating this area and not holding in your stomach or butt muscles.

3. Creating multiple neural pathways – why being able to get aroused and reach orgasm in different ways is important

As with any habit or behavior, our actions form connections in our brain called neural pathways. The more we repeat a behavior, the stronger that particular pathway becomes. In addition, the stronger the connection, the faster the brain cells communicate using that pathway. Think of it like going through a forest from one side to the other. The first time there is no path – it's just thick bushes, vines and trees. You need a machete to whack your way through and carve a path for yourself. But after doing that, the next time you go through you can see where you're going, you might only need to cut a few things back and you're able to walk through a lot faster. Each time you walk from one side to the other, it becomes easier. There is space around your body to walk (or even run) and the ground becomes flattened more and more. Over time, the ground even gets an indentation from your running back and forth. This creating and strengthening pathways is part of the learning process in the brain and also explains how we get better at the things we do regularly.

What does this have to do with masturbation you may ask? Well, it's common to develop a favorite way to masturbate to orgasm, but it's important to not get stuck with just one technique or path. Many people develop a style of masturbation that works for them and at some point stop exploring and playing creatively. Specific details for each person's favorite style will include whether they use a sex toy or fingers as well as things like the pressure and patterns of movement. Also what people mentally focus on will be part of their preferred process – whether they mainly focus on their bodily sensations, watch porn or play a fantasy in their head. Whatever we do, we create a neural pathway of the specific steps taken, which gets strengthened with each

192

time we masturbate that way. The stronger a single neural pathway becomes, the harder it become to orgasm with other styles of masturbating. To build and maintain flexibility in our sexual expression, it's useful to find multiple ways you can bring yourself to orgasm and thus have multiple neural pathways.

A neural pathway of a specific masturbation process gets strengthened through the release of feel-good brain chemicals such as dopamine, oxytocin and serotonin when we orgasm. Things can become problematic if someone has only one neural pathway that they discover is incompatible with other situations where they also want to get aroused and have an orgasm. This is why we benefit a lot from having multiple neural pathways. Let's look at some scenarios.

Imagine someone watches porn while they masturbate. Just to clarify, I don't think watching porn, in itself, is a problem. There are ethical issues to do with how a lot of mainstream porn is produced, which is why I recommend accessing ethically produced, feminist porn (refer to Resources at the end of this book). What can, however become a problem is the way we watch porn.

Imagine someone who likes to masturbate while watching porn. They may flick through multiple videos as their arousal builds. This masturbation style creates and reinforces a neural pathway, which links arousal and orgasm to novelty and a high level of mental stimulation. Someone who only has this pathway to arousal may find it hard to focus during intimacy with another person or find it more of a challenge to give themselves an orgasm if they can't access the Internet.

What about someone who uses their vibrator in a certain way, and only that way to orgasm. Whether they hold or rub it against their clitoris, insert it with or without other stimulation, if they do the same thing each time they're creating a well trodden path. Can you guess when having this single pathway might cause frustration? It's not the vibrator that's the problem, but one possibility is that they haven't created a pathway for getting aroused by touching themselves with their fingers, which may or may not limit them at some stage.

Sometimes the limitation is created by the body position. If you only ever masturbate in one position you might be creating a pathway that is incompatible with partner sex. For example, if you only ever masturbate lying with your legs clamped hard together, this creates a neural pathway connected to pressure of the legs together and possibly body tension in other muscles as well. Once again, that in itself isn't a problem, unless it's the only way you can get aroused and you feel limited by it at some stage.

What if you create elaborate fantasies that require deep concentration when you masturbate? Again, nothing's wrong with that in itself. But if it's your only method of turning yourself on then your pathway may be limited to being connected to the story in your head more than what is happening in the moment.

Reading through these scenarios I really hope you understand that I'm not saying anything is wrong with the above styles of masturbation. Each one is representative of a method that lots of people use and can be a tried and true strategy for turning yourself on and giving yourself an orgasm. I do, however, want you to realize the benefit of creating multiple pathways to arousal and orgasm. The more varied your options, the more flexibility you have to increase your sexual arousal. So mix up your sexual play every now and then and expand your repertoire for the benefit of getting out of a sexual rut as well as simply for the love of having multiple options! Having numerous options for arousal and orgasm can also be beneficial as a future back up if for any reason such as circumstances, injury or age means that you can no longer use one of your favorite techniques.

So how do you create multiple pathways? The key thing is to start mixing up whatever you're doing currently in your masturbation play. I've included loads of different exercises throughout this book for this purpose. If you use porn while masturbating, start playing away from the computer every now and then. If you normally flick through lots of videos, reduce the amount and even practice masturbating from start to end watching only one video. Have a play with creating the scenes in your head instead of watching them on screen. If you enjoy fantasizing while masturbating, practice being mindful to the physical sensations in your body and replace the visual movie in your mind with 'watching' or feeling the movements you're making instead. If you have a particular position you are always in when you masturbate, try out different positions and take the time to allow your brain to create a new neural pathway that connects your arousal with the new position. If you normally come quickly, explore edging (delaying an orgasm – more about that in Chapter 5: Practicing Pleasure) and drawing out the whole experience from start to finish. If you normally take lots of time, explore toys that decrease the arousal to orgasm time such as a vibrator or other clitoral stimulator.

Over time, the aim is to create multiple pathways of pleasure. Be aware that creating a new pathway generally takes time and patience, so be nice to yourself while you're creating it and remember to dedicate time to exploring and practicing new techniques.

4. Mental masturbation

You may think this is an odd concept, but the power of your mind can play a significant role in arousal. Mental masturbation is a creative way to add excitement and arousal to all of your sexual experiences as well as a way to connect to your sexuality in general. Were you aware that 2% of women can orgasm through fantasy alone? While that might not be many of us, even if you're one of the other 98%, what you do in the privacy of your own mind can be an additional technique of stoking your sexual flame of desire and arousal. I use the term mental masturbation here to include fantasizing as well as literally imagining you are masturbating when you are not.

Think of romantic and erotic scenes from movies and books that you find a turn-on. Put some thought into it and you'll probably also remember sexually-charged memories from your past, juicy stories you've heard from friends as well as fantasies of what you would like to experience. It's common to have sexual thoughts and desires and even to fantasize about things that you might not want or be able to experience in real life.

The interesting thing with imagining something in our mind is that the body often responds as if it is actually happening. Anyone who's scared of spiders or mice and have had their body shudder when someone told a story about having one run past or crawl across their skin knows exactly what I'm talking about. It doesn't matter that there is no spider or mouse in the room, just imagining it means the body reacts. You may even have cringed or shuddered just reading the last few sentences if you don't like spiders or mice!

It's the same with any other experience. Constantly stressing and thinking anxious thoughts about something can lead to pain and headaches, for example. But what about good or neutral thoughts?

Have you heard of the 'imagine a lemon' example? This is where you imagine a juicy, ripe lemon. Go ahead and imagine one now in front of you. Visualize what it looks like and bring to mind the citrus smell that would be released if you dig your nails into the peel. If you cut into the fruit, you know what the juice would look like

196

that gathers underneath and if you fully imagine taking a segment of the lemon now and biting into it (go ahead, really imagine that sour taste filling your mouth), you can also imagine the taste of that bitterness filling your mouth and notice how your mouth would pucker.

Now check your mouth. If you've vividly imagined those details about the lemon and its taste, you've probably got more saliva in your mouth now. But there is no lemon. You've literally got your saliva flowing simply by going through the sensual experience in your mind.

And this is where the possibilities become endless. What turns you on? What have you not even experienced in real life but find extremely erotic to think about? It could be a general scenario, a specific sexual act or a full story line. Even if it is literally or technically impossible, if it's a turn on and you allow yourself to imagine it... fully imagine it in sensory detail, then your body is likely to respond sooner or later.

Time to play:

<u>Fantasy land</u>

Grab your notebook and start by writing a list of your fantasies. The list might include things you actually want to experience one day, memories, made up and mythical scenes, and things you wouldn't dream of doing in real life. Give yourself permission to do a brain-dump of the ideas that come to mind. If you want some help to explore fantasies that might turn you on, I suggest you delve into the interviews and letters shared by women in books such as *Garden of Desires: The Evolution of Women's Sexual Fantasies* curated by Emily Dubberly or Nancy Friday's books on the same topic. These books and others like them, explore uncensored personal sexual fantasies, taboos, desires and women's most private sexual thoughts.

According to many surveys, the most common female fantasies include themes of:

– Passion, intimacy and romance
– Novelty, adventure and variety (e.g. sex with a stranger or in an unusual setting)
– BDSM (bondage, discipline, dominance, submission, sadism, masochism)
– Multiple partner sex such as threesomes or orgies
– Swinging, polyamory and open relationships
– Sexual taboos and 'forbidden' acts
– Sex with a female (among women identifying as heterosexual)
– Gender and sexual fluidity (e.g. cross-dressing, having sex as a male)

These are just some of the common themes and by no means does this list cover the full range of women's fantasies. You can use the above list to spark a fantasy in your mind if you haven't already got one you can think of.

Variation 1

Just as you would for a meditation or mindfulness exercise, gift yourself some time to fully immerse yourself in the experience of your fantasy. A time when you won't be distracted and in a place that is comfortable and where you can relax without disruptions. Is there a particular song that fits the mood of the fantasy you are exploring? If so, put it on and notice how your fantasy experience and arousal are heightened.

Start by setting the scene. Where are you? Are you alone or with someone else? Create the scene in your mind as a film director would. Fill in as much detail as you can as you play the scene or story line in your mind. Notice the sensory input of your fantasy – what do you see, feel (touch as well as emotions), smell, taste and hear? As you build the scene, notice you can replay certain scenes, zoom in or zoom out. You can even play around with perspective – seeing yourself from the outside as if you are an observer then compare that with imagining being in your body and seeing it all through your own eyes.

Notice some of the key elements of what really turns you on in your fantasy and realize how you can create other fantasies using the same theme. For example, let's say you have a fantasy of being on a tropical island having sex with someone you've just met who's sole focus is to give you maximum pleasure. If the part that really stands out as a turn on is that it's sex with a stranger, you can transport that theme into endless backdrops whether at a friend's party, sex club, at home, with a professional escort, on a plane... the options are endless. Or let's say the key turn on is that it's all about someone only wanting to give you sexual pleasure. In that case, you could once again simply change the setting or character or jump into a complete made up world where you are a goddess being pleasured by many attractive admirers all stroking your body as you lie on an enormous bed with a soft canopy floating in the breeze. Get the picture?

Variation 2

Bring up elements of your fantasy during the day. Most people daydream at certain points during the day anyway, so why not give yourself something pleasurable to think about! It might only be for a couple of minutes that you play back a certain scene in your mind but after doing so, notice how it affects your levels of arousal and interest in sex or masturbation for later when you get home.

Variation 3

Erotic writing is another way to explore your fantasies. This is a way in which you can bring a fantasy to life or even allow yourself to discover a new fantasy's storyline by seeing where your mind takes you as you write. Simply grab your preferred writing tool, whether device or pen and paper, and allow your creativity to run free. You might discover that writing helps you understand more about your fantasies. You might also experience writing as a way to boost your arousal and empower yourself sexually.

Replay

An easy starting point for mental masturbation is taking your own sexual experiences and replaying them in your head. You may not like elaborate story lines and would rather focus on certain moves like being held tight during sex, having your clitoris licked, having your hair brushed off your face or looking deeply into a partner's eyes. Whatever you enjoy or have enjoyed in the past can be taken as subject matter for your mental masturbation. It doesn't matter if it happened to you recently or 20 years ago. Recall the memory, step into your body in the memory, feel, see, hear and breathe it all in again. Allow yourself to sink into the sensations fully.

Using replay as a mental masturbation technique can also be a way to get yourself in the mood before a date or night with a partner. Lots of women say they need a bit of warm-up time to get into the mood for sex but limit themselves if they only ever wait for their partner to initiate foreplay. Playing your favorite sexual scenes in your mind allows you to firstly take control of your arousal and secondly could provide some content for sending a sexy message to your partner mid-day about being turned on while imagining having sex. Sharing what you're looking forward to with a partner might trigger sexual thoughts in their mind of that scene as well, increasing the chance of you recreating that scene in real life once you are together. If you've been in a long term relationship, an useful source of sexual inspiration is remembering some of your first sexual moments together – the first touches, the first time undressing – seeing and feeling each other's bodies.

Anticipate

A common fantasy, which is experienced automatically when people are in the first exciting stages of a relationship or dating, is an anticipation scene. The heady mix of brain chemicals and hormones racing through our bodies in those early days makes us lose track of what we're doing and focuses our attention on our desire. As we anticipate the next time we'll see and feel our new lust or love interest, the imagined scene and sensations can significantly increase our sexual energy, thoughts and arousal. The heart races just imagining seeing the person or imagining the feeling of their hand brushing across our hand or thigh.

As a relationship progresses and stabilizes over time, people often stop doing this mental process of anticipating. Or they only use this powerful strategy to enhance negative emotions and experiences by replaying and anticipating arguments, rejection and remembering moments of not feeling valued or loved. I encourage you to choose to reclaim anticipation for hot memories as well as positive loving ones. The future hasn't happened yet, so if you're going to make stuff up in your mind about it, you may as well choose some positive scenes!

Note: If you're in a relationship and you notice you've gotten into the habit of replaying and anticipating mostly negative experiences with your partner, I encourage you to seek a therapist to help you work through the challenges and past hurts in your relationship as well as consider the approach of EFT (Emotionally Focused Couples Therapy) to help bring you closer and heal together.

Add on

Next time you're masturbating, add on a fantasy story line with you as the main character. For example, if you're masturbating with your fingers, you could imagine that your lover is in the room watching you and being aroused by seeing you pleasure yourself. Or you could imagine it's your lover's finger or tongue that is softly brushing past your clitoris rather than your finger.

If you have the sun on your skin while masturbating, you could close your eyes and imagine you're lounging on a private yacht in tropical turquoise water. If you want to get really into it, you could play some gentle wave sounds in the background.

If you are masturbating using toys, then you could picture yourself being taught how to use them by someone you find hot. Or you could imagine you're testing them as part of research with or without the researchers in the room with you.

If your form of masturbation is rubbing yourself against something like a pillow, then a simple add-on is to imagine that you are on top of and rubbing onto a partner or take your add-on further by imagining you're having penetrative sex even if you are just stimulating your clitoris. The sensations can be heightened by practicing Autogenic Training (see in the next chapter).

5. Practicing pleasure

Mindfulness and meditation

The concept of mindfulness simply means choosing to bring your attention and awareness to the here and now – with non-judgment, curiosity and acceptance. This is the basic foundation of mindfulness and it is from this starting point that many exercises have been developed around the world.

When it comes to female sexuality and arousal, mindfulness is extremely important. This is true regardless of whether you are wanting to experience pleasure by yourself or with a partner. Whats more, it applies not just to sexual, but to any pleasure. Many of us have had the experience of finding it hard to focus on pleasure, to enjoy the moment and relax – because our minds are wandering off thinking about work, future plans or other responsibilities.

A study looking at the relationship between mindfulness and sexual arousal in women, made a number of significant discoveries. Three groups of women were shown erotic material and monitored for physical signs of sexual arousal. The level of their arousal was measured by recording changes of vasocongestion in the vagina (swelling of body tissues due to increased blood flow to the area). The women in one group were asked to notice non-genital changes in their body that related to being aroused, such as any increase in heart rate, erection of nipples, swelling of breasts and tension in muscles. The women in the second group were instructed to notice genital signs of arousal, such as tension in vaginal muscles, a feeling of warmth in the pelvic region and lubrication in the vagina. The third group acted as a control group and were thus given no instructions.

After viewing the erotic material, all women were asked to report on how aroused they felt. Their self-reports were then compared with the measured physical levels of arousal. Both the first and second groups who had paid attention to physical signs of arousal reported feeling aroused and were more aligned with the recorded physiological changes. In contrast, the third group had a much lower feeling of arousal despite the fact they were actually physiologically aroused, as shown by their levels of vasocongestion.

These really interesting results of the study highlight just how vital it is that a woman has conscious awareness of her body, its responses and signs of arousal. I have worked with a number of women who have told me they don't think they get aroused when their partner touches them or when they have sex. On further questioning, we discovered that they weren't even aware of the signs that would tell them they are aroused in the first place. They were unaware that their body was responding with a state of arousal, simply because they were preoccupied with other thoughts.

So to put it in really simple language: The more in touch you are with your body, its responses and signals of arousal, the more likely it is you will feel aroused as a result of mental and physical stimulation.

Therefore you have two possible tasks if you would like to improve in this area. Firstly, it is recommended that you practice bringing your attention to the present moment. At any given moment, practice focusing on your sensory experiences in the now – not just during sex or self-pleasuring, but at any point during the day. Pay attention to what you hear, feel, see, smell and taste. If your mind drifts off to a thought or emotion, simply bring your focus back to something that is in the now. Try this exercise now as you're reading. What else are you aware of? What sounds can you hear in the background? What things can you see around you? How does your body feel? Can you taste or smell anything?

Secondly, practice integrating mindfulness into your sexual experiences to increase awareness of your arousal. This will also help increase your comfort as a sensual and sexual being as you become more attuned with your body. Pay attention to how it feels as you become lubricated, the sensation of your nipples against the material of your top, your pelvic floor muscles tightening and releasing, any increase in your heart rate, skin flushing and pleasurable, involuntary shudders. You will get more pleasure over time the more you fully inhabit your body and its sensations.

If you already struggle to take time out for yourself during a busy day, then this might be an indication that you would benefit from integrating some form of mindfulness into your day. – even if only in a small way at first. You see, people are often running around in their mind constantly jumping from thought to thought, from the future to the past and back again at top speed, and hardly ever really stopping to enjoy the present moment. When we learn to stay in the moment, we can notice not only the feelings in our bodies, but also the many positive and beautiful things that are happening around us.

You can improve your ability to be mindful by learning meditation. You can also start by just paying attention to your sensory input at any given moment. Here are some simple things you can practice noticing every day:

– Birdsong.
– Leaves and nature: The variety of colors and shades and any movement in the breeze.
– People around you: Notice smiles, eye colors and unique details of people's faces.
– The weather: The feeling of raindrops landing and sliding down your skin, the sun on your face, the feeling on your scalp as your hair is blowing in the wind.
– Food: Its smell, the texture in your mouth, the complexities of flavors.

– Any tension in your body and how it feels as you allow yourself to release it and relax.
– Noticing your feet on the ground while walking or standing.
– Feeling your back resting against a chair.
– Noticing the air as it passes through your nostrils – cooler on the way in and warmer on the way out.
– Checking if you can feel your heartbeat/pulse anywhere in your body.

Time to play:

<u>Body scan – Tuning in to your body</u>

The purpose and benefit of learning to tune in to our bodies, emotions, thoughts and physical sensations is that our self-awareness increases. Having self-awareness means that we gain more power over being able to identify emotions, self-judgment and limiting beliefs. With practice, we learn to simply observe emotions and thoughts without feeling pulled along by them. We become more skilled at directing our focus to where we want it to be. Self-awareness also empowers us sexually by enabling us to create a connection with our levels of arousal – mentally, physically and emotionally.

Take a comfortable seated or lying down position. Ensure you are warm and that you will not be interrupted for at least 10 minutes.

Take three deep breaths to bring your attention into your body. Allow yourself to take time out from your day and tune in with yourself.

Before you do the body scan, notice how your body and mind feel overall. Imagine yourself taking a mental snapshot of your mood, energy levels and predominant thoughts. Without judgment, notice whatever it is that you notice and breathe deeply.

Starting at your feet, simply notice how they feel. If you

are wearing shoes or socks, notice how the material feels against the sides of your feet, along the top and sole of each foot. If you have bare feet, feel the air on your skin, or the material against them if you have them covered by a blanket. Does one foot feel more relaxed than the other?

Moving up, tune into your calves and then your thighs. Connect in with the feelings of both the backs and front of your legs and allow them to rest down with gravity. Feel the insides of your legs and also notice just as you did with your feet, how any material or air feels against your skin.

Bring your attention to your pelvis. Can you bring your awareness into any sensations in your vagina, vulva, clitoris and anus? Take a moment to rest your focus in the pelvic area and notice if clenching and releasing your pelvic floor muscles a couple of times helps you identify and connect in more clearly with this area. Notice also if doing this brings up any emotions, sensations or thoughts. If anything challenging comes up at any time, direct your focus back to your breath and remind yourself that you are in control. I encourage you to be gentle and loving with yourself as you do this exercise.

You may notice that focusing on your pelvic area increases your awareness of any pleasurable sensations or arousal. Again, just notice what you notice with gentle awareness.

Bring your attention up to your waist and core. Feel the skin here against the material of your clothes. Feel your belly rise and fall with every breath. Notice how your back feels. If you feel discomfort anywhere, aim to observe it without judgment.

Move your focus up to your ribs and up to your breasts. Can you feel the curve of your breasts against the material of the top you are wearing? Tune in to any sensations and feel your breath rising and falling in your chest. Bring your attention also up from your lower back to the middle and then top of your back.

Now, notice sensations in your fingers and hands. Scan this area. Notice the temperature of your hands and any other sensations you may be feeling in them. Feel how you can really focus on each individual finger on each hand and the skin between the fingers. Move your attention up one wrist, along the arm to the shoulder and then up the other arm from the hand to the wrist to the shoulder. Feel the sensations in each shoulder. Can you allow them to sink down with gravity?

Bring your attention to your neck. Notice any difference in sensations between the front and the back of your neck. If you hold tension in this area you could benefit from giving your neck a gentle and slow stretch by bringing your head towards one shoulder and then the other while taking some deep breaths.

And now tune into the feelings in and on your face. How relaxed are your facial muscles? Is your forehead clenched or relaxed? Are your eyes resting under heavy eyelids or straining in any way? Is your jaw unlocked and free? Notice how your scalp feels.

To bring this scan to completion, take another sweeping scan of your whole body just like you did at the start. How are you feeling? What are your thoughts? What sensations are you aware of in your body? And how different do you feel now compared to at the start?

Savoring

A particularly useful exercise to practice is the art of savoring. The more you practice this, the more you can bring the same mindset into sex and intimacy and reap the rewards of more connectivity with yourself (and a partner).

Example 1: The shower

The next time you have a shower, choose to bring your focus fully to what you are experiencing (rather than thoughts about the day or what happened earlier). Connect in with your senses and really savor the experience.

With your head under the shower head, notice how it feels as the water lands on your scalp. Follow the flow of water as it trickles down your scalp, down your neck, along your back and front, along your legs and the feeling of your feet as the water flows past them into the drain.

Breathe in the warm steam. Feel the warmth and humidity in your nostrils and the sensation of breathing in the warm air. You might like to choose a favorite essential oil or shower product with a pleasant scent to enjoy rubbing into your hair or body and breathing in the smell as it gets released.

Close your eyes and stand with the spray directed at your face as you slowly breathe out. As you do this, tune into the sensation of the gentle patter of water around your face and the water trickling down. Notice how your muscles feel in the warm water. Listen to the sound.

What else can you notice and enjoy as you savor the moment?

Example 2: Hot drink

Make or buy yourself a favorite hot drink. Literally, take a moment now to get a hot drink in front of you or return to this exercise later. Sit with nothing else to do except sipping your drink. No doubt there have been plenty of times where you have simply gulped this drink back without any thought or connecting with the experience. Or you have mindlessly drunk it as your thoughts have wandered off to chores and worry about your life.

So today I encourage you to sit and experience focusing on just drinking your drink. Taking the time to do this slowly – to enjoy it and savor the moment.

Take the cup in your hands and feel the temperature. Close your eyes and breathe in its scent. Notice if you are salivating more in anticipation of this drink. Look at what color it is and if there are any patterns (like a swirl on top of a coffee's milk foam or colors seeping out of a tea bag). Take a moment to feel the texture of the cup it is in and the color of the glass, pottery or whatever material it is made of. Rub your fingers over the cup.

Now take a tiny sip and without swallowing just yet, let the flavor fill your mouth and notice where in your mouth you get the various taste sensations. Allow the liquid to slide down your throat and notice the sensation as it does.

Continue savoring your drink like this as you drink the whole cup slowly. Part of your savoring experience might also be enjoying other experiences around you such as the flickering light and warmth from a fireplace, some sun on your skin or listening to background sounds.

When your mind wanders during this and other mindfulness exercises (as it is bound to do), simply bring it back to the experience. It is highly likely you will have to bring your attention back numerous times – that is fine and completely normal! The mind likes to wander, and every time you choose to bring it back to whatever it is that you choose to focus on, you are strengthening your ability to do so.

<u>15-minute clitoral massage</u>

There is a 15-minute clitoral orgasm method described by Tim Ferriss in his book *The 4-Hour Body* and taught by the organization One Taste, which teaches it as part of an orgasmic meditation method with a partner. This super soft way of touching the clitoris is a simple technique to combine mindfulness and the savoring of sexual arousal. I have adapted the method here for self-pleasuring.

Set aside time, either first thing in the morning, before you go to sleep, or during the day. Use a timer with a gentle finish sound (e.g. bell or peaceful music) to let you know when the 15 minutes are up.

Before you begin, you might like to set an intention for your practice such as the following:

– To ground yourself – bringing your focus out of your mind and into your body.
– To explore your sexual arousal.
– To become more aware of sensations in your body.
– To increase self-love and acceptance.

These four intentions are just ideas to start you thinking. Pick an intention that resonates with you.

Lie on a comfortable surface with cushions as needed to support you. Explore this meditative exercise with legs resting slightly apart or bent at the knees and opening out to the sides (support your legs if needed with cushions).

Gently pull up and hold the clitoral hood with your left hand (or right if you are left-handed). You are going to be making feather-light micro movements on the 'upper left quadrant' of your clitoral head. To identify this point, imagine a clock face with 12 at the bottom of your clitoris (closest to your vaginal opening) and 6 at the top (the part covered by the hood). Your upper quadrant is at the 7 o'clock point – a little to the left side.

With the tip of a finger on your right hand, start making soft, gentle strokes in this 7pm spot (in the small indentation between clitoris and hood). Continue these soft strokes at a speed that is enjoyable and allows you to focus on the pleasure that fills your body. Lean more towards a slow stroke rather than a fast one. Give this soft touch your full attention for the full 15 minutes.

When your mind wanders, which it will (remember that's completely normal), just bring your attention back to your touch and the sensations you are experiencing in your body. There is no goal or outcome to be aiming for with this and other mindfulness exercises. Incorporating mindfulness as a daily habit helps train your brain to focus on a chosen experience without judgment. This helps increase feelings and responses of calm, acceptance, enjoyment and resilience. In the context of sexuality, it can increase levels of arousal, enjoyment of sex and intimacy and help you stay present. Practicing this clitoral massage is just one way you can do this.

When the time is up, don't jump up immediately. Instead, keep your eyes closed and stay tuned in with your body for at least a few deep breaths. This may even become a favorite part of the exercise as you give yourself time to enjoy the sexual energy running through your body.

Note: You can choose to either let the sexual arousal ease off after this exercise or continue touch until orgasm. If you choose the latter, then I recommend that you consciously end the mindfulness exercise before continuing, so that you preserve the goal-free nature of the exercise in your mind.

I encourage you to practice clitoral touch regularly as a meditation exercise with the aim of connecting in with and awakening your sexual self without seeking an orgasm. It will be particularly beneficial to people who get caught up in thinking during sex and want to learn how to focus more on their bodily sensations.

Autogenic training (A.T.)

I first came across Autogenic Training in Germany (German: Autogenes Training) where it was a popular therapy taught for inducing a state of relaxation – to reduce stress and help treat some health conditions. Autogenic training is similar to self-hypnosis in that practitioners mentally repeat suggestions to themselves in order to create a specific state of mind that impacts the body in a positive way.

Exercises include scanning the body and making suggestions such as that parts of the body are becoming heavy, relaxed and warm as well as imagining feeling at peace. Officially learning AT requires dedication, time and practice. One of the initial exercises often focuses simply on making the hands and arms feel heavy. If you want to master AT, it is recommended that you learn from a trained therapist.

For the purposes of this book, however, I'm going to teach you a simple exercise that integrates elements of AT and self-hypnosis to enhance your sexual enjoyment. If you want to explore further, look for a comprehensive training online or in your area.

Time to play:

Warm and relaxed

Lying down in a warm and comfortable room, begin by tuning in to the feelings in your body. Scan your body and notice any areas of discomfort as well as areas of comfort and relaxation. Make sure to take good care of

213

your body as you do this exercise; leave out any injured muscles from the following clench-and-release process.

Next, you're going to clench and then release your muscles from the toes up just as you would in progressive muscle relaxation. Breathe in as you squeeze the muscle and breathe out as you release it. At the same time as relaxing each muscle, tell yourself that you are relaxing and letting go. Literally say to yourself in your mind with every muscle release: "Relaxing and letting go".

Start by clenching and releasing your feet muscles – "Relaxing and letting go", then your leg muscles – "Relaxing and letting go". Move on to your pelvic area and core muscles and finish up with clenching and releasing your hands, arms, shoulders, neck and face muscles. With each out-breath, silently repeat the phrase "Relaxing and letting go" to yourself.

Allow yourself time to slowly go through the muscles like this with the aim of creating a feeling of relaxation and calm throughout your whole body.

Next, focus your attention on the sensations in your pelvis. Engage with your vagina by squeezing your pelvic floor muscles and tell yourself: "Warm and relaxed" as you breathe out and relax them again. Tune in to the sensations you feel in your vagina, clitoris, and vulva. If you aren't noticing any, simply continue focusing on this area with curiosity.

As you connect in with your vagina, continue noticing any sensations you feel while gently repeating the suggestion "Warm and relaxed" with every out-breath. After a few minutes of doing this, feel free to extend your awareness to other sensual parts of your body such as your nipples and inner thighs, while repeating the suggestion "Warm and relaxed."

You don't have to do this exercise for long. Even 5-10 minutes is enough. However, the more frequently you

214

tune in to these areas of your body with the "Relaxed and letting go" and "Warm and relaxed" suggestions, the more your awareness and sensations will grow over time. AT courses recommend practicing the exercises multiple times a day.

As you become more and more attuned to your body and your ability to heighten physical sensations, you can play around with the process. What other suggestions can you think of that you would like to explore? What about "Aroused and sensitive", or "Free and alive" ? The more you practice awakening a chosen state of body and mind, the more you can tap into it before or during masturbation and sex to increase awareness and sensitivity and thus intensify every moment including the orgasm. Remember though – it is through dedicated practice that you will gain the skill.

Enhancing pleasure through breath and visualization

There are many spiritual and sensual practices that put a lot of focus on the art of correct breathing and the breath in general. Using your breath, you can increase sensations by focusing on energy flowing through your body as you breathe in and out. Deep, diaphragmatic breathing (all the way down to your belly) is recommended and something you may have to learn first if your breath is typically shallow and restricted to the chest. You can discover more about using breath to increase sexual pleasure and deepen your experience – even taking your sexual experiences into the realm of spiritual experiences by delving more into practices such as Tantra and Kama Sutra.

215

Time to play:

Expanding sexual energy

Before you do this visualization, bring yourself to sexual arousal beyond the initial warm-up phase, but not yet to climax. Get to the stage where your genital area feels warm and aroused and you strongly desire continued stimulation to orgasm. Some people find that calming meditation music assists with visualizations. If you want to explore this yourself, choose a song that is long, peaceful, and has a positive vibe. Play it at a comfortable volume in the background.

Lying on your back, place a hand on your belly and one on your chest and take a few deep breaths. You should feel the hand on your belly rising with the air as it deeply fills your lungs and the diaphragm muscle moves with your breath. If you don't feel your belly rising, take a moment to allow your breathing to deepen in this way.

Next, without giving yourself direct sexual stimulation, bring your mind's focus to your pelvis and sensations inside your vagina as well as outside on your vulva. Feel any energy, warmth, and desire for touch on the skin or in the muscles. Tune in to your bodily sensations in this moment.

Now, imagine a colored ball of sexual energy in your vagina. Pick a color that represents sexual energy for you in this moment. As you breathe in, imagine breathing in energy that with every out-breath you send down into your vagina. With each breath, imagine the colored ball of sexual energy you're sending to your vagina expanding.

As the ball of energy grows, imagine it spreading beyond the pelvis, growing more and more. Enjoy spreading it with every breath to fill more of your body; reaching down your legs and up into your chest. Keep breathing deeply, allowing yourself to focus on visualizing the expansion of the sexual energy to eventually fill all of you from the top of your head to the tip of your toes until your whole body is surrounded by this ball of sexual energy. Give yourself time to visualize this expansion.

The color might shift as it expands or it might stay the same. You might choose to expand the energy just within your body or have it expand out so you are resting in the middle of a much larger circle of energy that encompasses your body. Just be curious and playful with what feels good for you as you do this exercise.

Flowing sexual energy throughout your body

As above, bring yourself first to a heightened sexual arousal. Choose a meditative song if you wish for the background to help heighten the following experience. Bring your breathing to a slow, deep pace.

Focus your attention on your physical sensations and signs of arousal. Notice how your body feels in this aroused state. Bring your awareness to any genital sensations as well as those throughout the rest of your body.

As with the previous exercise, imagine the sexual energy resting in your vagina having a color. It may be the same color as before or it might be a different one. It might change from day to day and alter in shade or stay exactly the same. For several breaths, imagine breathing directly into the energy ball to charge it.

Next, with a deep breath in, flow the energy up along the back of your spine and to the top of your head. As you release the breath back out, let the energy flow down across your face through your chest and back down to the bottom of your pelvis. Breathing in, flow the energy up the back of your spine. Breathing out, flow it down over your face, chest, core and to the pelvis. Breathing in, up the spine, breathing out, down in front to the pelvis.

Continue this circular flow of your sexual energy for a few minutes before continuing in your sexual play. Notice any changes in state (emotionally, physically, mentally, spiritually) and sensations following this exercise and the above expanding energy exercise. You may find it increases your focus, brings a sense of calm and gives you more of a full body experience. Or you might just feel more peaceful and in the moment.

Power up with edging

Edging is an orgasm control exercise some people swear by. To practice edging, you build up your arousal until you start approaching orgasm. Then you stop stimulation in order to let the arousal subside before building it back up again. This pulling back and building up is often repeated numerous times before allowing yourself to succumb to a powerful, orgasmic climax.

Why would you do this and how does it work? Edging is typically used as a method of intensifying orgasms. In fact, according to the women's sexual pleasure website and app, OMGYes, edging results in longer and more intense orgasms for 65.5% of women. Playing with edging can help you become really familiar with the specific sensations in the lead-up to orgasm as you experiment with the timing of pulling back. It helps extend the duration of being highly aroused. When used during partner sex, it can be part of a playful and teasing approach, for example "I'm not letting you come just yet", as well as take the focus away from aiming straight for orgasm.

Edging isn't for everyone though. Some people find edging just plain annoying or frustrating. But of course you won't know until you try for yourself.

Time to play:

<u>Just stop</u>

Bring yourself to near orgasm in whichever way you want and then as you feel it approaching, stop. Stop all movement and stimulation and allow the feelings to die down. Wait for a minute or two. Then start up again. You can play with how long you wait before building the arousal back up. As your arousal builds again and you feel yourself getting closer to coming, stop for a second time. Repeat a number of times until the desire for orgasm is so high that you don't want to wait any more.

<u>Change input</u>

If the idea of completely stopping isn't your cup of tea, try a more fluid edging version. Instead of stopping completely, in this variation you just switch to another pleasurable form of touch. This is where you have to know yourself well, because you don't want to pick an alternative movement that is so pleasurable that you orgasm anyway. Therefore, pick something pleasurable but less intense. Some examples of this could be switching from direct clitoral touch to circling your vaginal entrance, caressing your breasts instead, stroking your labia, or doing a much slower variation of the previous movement.

Enjoy the alternative touch as the impending orgasm fades away. Then, return to your original stimulation or something else that brings you close to orgasm again. As you approach climax, change the type of touch once again. Repeat easing off as often as you like.

Indulgent masturbation

Just as you might treat yourself to a massage or spa treatment once in a while, giving masturbation the feel of a spa day can turn it into a luxury indulgence. Whether you choose a lazy weekend day, midweek evening or other time, clear a few hours or more to indulge in your sexual desires.

This is the time to pamper your mind and body. There are no rules for how you are going to give yourself a delicious sexual experience and each time can be different. Depending on where you live and the time of year, you might go for a swim or have a soak in a bath with added bubbles, salts or essential oils. After that you could choose a moisturizing body cream or oil to rub into your skin. Do you like to dance, listen to music or sing? Perhaps you'll use those to connect with your sexuality. Maybe you'll play with some sex toys and give yourself time to luxuriate in taking your time and playing with edging. Do you have a sexy scene from a movie or porn site you want to watch? You could put on a film's soundtrack and create an elaborate fantasy in your mind with you as the lead character. If you're artistic, perhaps you're inspired to create something based on your desires. Maybe you find yourself researching the latest toy developments and imagine trying them for the first time. You could listen to and watch artistic visual representations of female orgasms on an orgasm sound library website (https://orgasmsoundlibrary.com/#gallery) and if you dare, submit one of your own to be shared with the world.

You can of course also choose to simply spend the time with no extra input at all; just yourself and the touch sensations you create with your hands and body. Whatever you do, do it with a sense of slow indulgence to make it the ultimate gift of sexual self-care.

Time to play:

<u>Day of sexual awareness</u>

Research shows that a large number of women are consciously unaware of their physical arousal and sexuality. For this exercise you are going to choose a day where you commit to tuning in to and noticing any signs of arousal or sensual sensations or thoughts. This is a day for consciously choosing to notice the sexual and sensual and enhance them through giving them your attention. You may or may not choose to masturbate on a day of sexual awareness. As always, it's your choice.

As Sexuality Consultant, Pamela Madsen worded it so fittingly: "Women learn to leave their bodies during sex and watch the reactions of lovers to their bodies instead of being curious about what else might give them pleasure instead of just being the object of desire. What becomes unfamiliar is feeling whole and beautiful in their own pleasure. Instead, the desire to be desired becomes the orgasm; the fetish and turn on. Sexual pleasure becomes encased in this constant reaching to be seen, desired and pleasing to everyone but themselves, because that is what they see everywhere. Women enjoying their bodies and their pleasure for their own desire is rare. What is needed is an entire re-wiring of erotic culture for women."

Therefore starting with just one day – choose to start re-wiring your erotic experience with yourself. Choose to let go of seeing yourself through the eyes of the other. See your eroticism through your own eyes – enjoy your body, explore pleasure and consciously choose to engage with the sensual and sexy.

6. Exercise and diet

Up to this point, we've covered a lot of information about techniques, toys, psychological and emotional aspects of arousal and understanding the role of various body parts in helping us get turned on and have great orgasms. Something we haven't looked at yet, however, is the role our physical health plays.

Arousal and orgasms require a healthy body. We're complex beings. Having a healthy heart, healthy skin, healthy blood vessels and healthy nerves is required for sexual arousal and orgasm. In addition, we need sufficient levels of the neurotransmitter nitric oxide, a balance between parasympathetic and sympathetic nervous system activation and healthy hormone balance. Our sexual health can be affected by the side effects of medications, cancer treatments, limited mobility and untreated pain.

We have a lot of influence over our health. Not always, but often a lot more than people think. In addition, a healthy lifestyle plays an important role in preventative healthcare. We can assist our bodies to be able to access and sustain arousal by living a sex-healthy lifestyle. The two areas I'm going to cover here are exercise and diet.

Exercise

Humans have evolved to move rather than blob on the couch or sit on an office chair, even though that's where a lot of us spend hours each day. There are multiple body systems that benefit from movement and exercise. One of the key points to remember is that arousal is a cardiovascular event, thus requires ease of blood flow throughout our body. Earlier in the book, I referred to Ellen Barnard at A Women's Touch mentioning research which revealed that women over 60 experience a 36%

222

increase in sexual satisfaction due to something as basic as a 15-minute walk before sex. It's a simple fact that looking after your heart's health and exercising it directly benefits your sexual health. A sex-healthy lifestyle is also one with low levels of inflammation. Exercise is one of the ways we can create an anti-inflammatory response in the body.

Exercise also affects our hormones. One of those affected is testosterone. Testosterone is present in the female body to varying degrees and its levels increase after exercise. That's great when it comes to arousal, because testosterone contributes to our ability to feel desire. For someone experiencing low desire and wanting to give it a boost, the effect exercise has on testosterone is a great motivator to get moving.

Many people also talk about using exercise as a way to let go of the day's stress and that's important too, because arousal becomes so much harder to make happen if we're not able to let go and relax. Being able to easily move between arousal and relaxation depends on the activation of the parasympathetic and sympathetic nervous systems. And this is also positively affected by exercise.

Nitric oxide (NO) is something you probably don't hear much about but it's as important to us as oxygen. Nitric oxide is made by healthy blood vessel walls and healthy neurons. It in turn also helps keep the vessels and neurons healthy. Among its numerous functions is helping information about our arousal flow through our nerves. Nitric oxide is also required for the engorgement of our erectile tissues (i.e. the clitoris). Exercise plays a key part in keeping our levels of nitric oxide in balance.

The main thing about exercise is to find something you enjoy and have a regular routine. What can help for lots of people is creating a sense of accountability by doing it with a friend. The social aspect can also make the experience more fun. If you can't find a friend to exercise with, then joining a group can be another option. If your motivation needs a boost, experiment with combining exercise with something you really enjoy. For example, make a deal with yourself that you only listen to your favorite podcast while going for a walk or jog. A combo deal like this that has often worked for me is doing resistance training with weights as I watch the next episode of a series. Dancing is another favorite of mine, even if it is just me jumping around in the kitchen while I wait for the pot to boil. Find your enjoyable activities to combine with movement. Exercising doesn't mean you have to join a gym or do team sports unless that's interesting for you.

Remember to also find lots of ways to incorporate what's called incidental activity (aka accidental exercise) into your life. Take the stairs, park or get off the bus a little further away so you get an extra walk, carry your groceries, cut your own vegetables, throw a ball with someone, walk to ask a colleague a question in the office rather than emailing them, pull out weeds, and sit on the floor every now and then. In the back of your mind, ask yourself: "How can I get a little more movement right now?"

If you are new to exercise or have had a long break, I recommend seeking professional advice before embarking on a new exercise program.

Diet

If you're committed to prioritizing sexual expression, it's important to consider it from a holistic point of view. This includes eating a diet that promotes healthy sexual functioning. Because arousal and orgasms are cardiovascular events, a good sex diet needs to also be a heart-healthy one.

Once again, we're seeking general health, because if we don't, our sex life can be affected negatively. For example, if we have poor artery health, our blood can't flow as easily to our sex organs, high cholesterol and high blood pressure leads to less lubrication, arousal, fewer orgasms and lower satisfaction. We want to have low levels of inflammation in our bodies to support them to function the way they were designed to.

What's a sex healthy diet that's low in inflammation? It's often referred to as the Mediterranean diet. Meals focus on high amounts of whole-food, plant-based ingredients. Therefore, we want to base our meals around vegetables, fruits, legumes, whole grains and healthy fat sources like nuts. Animal products including meat are eaten in much smaller quantities than in the typical Western diet. Processed foods are ideally avoided completely.

Dr Greger at Nutritionfacts.org takes it a step further and suggests a purely whole-food, plant-based diet with minimal to no animal foods. Of course, what we eat is a personal choice but I am impressed with the integrity of Dr Greger's work. His mission is to review all available research to help the public get evidence-based advice in a world that sometimes feels very confusing when it comes to what food we should and shouldn't be eating for optimal health.

Remember nitric oxide's vital role in sexual functioning? Nitric oxide is made by healthy blood vessel walls and healthy neurons but it is synthesized from L-arginine and calcium. A couple of sources of L-arginine are nuts and whole grains. Plant-based sources of calcium include legumes – that is lentils, black beans, chickpeas and so on, as well as leafy greens and carrots.

Depending on your current diet, switching to a more plant-based diet might seem a big task. If that's the case, as with all big goals, break it down into small steps. A good place to start is to increase the amounts and variety of fruit and vegetables that you eat with each meal.

The bonus in all of this is that if you make healthy changes to your diet and increase your levels of physical activity, your overall health will benefit.

PART FIVE: YOUR PERSONAL PROFILE & CONCLUDING INFORMATION

My aim with this book has been to guide you in a journey of sexual discovery. I hope to have shed light on how arousal works in both the mind and body as well as encouraged you to try out many new moves, techniques, experiences and toys. I hope it has been a rich and fun experience and one that has helped you identify some key moves that give you immense pleasure and give you permission to continue exploring your sexual pleasure at any age.

1. Self-exploration questions

The next step is to take some time to reflect back on the journey you have been on while reading this book. I realize that some will read this book slowly doing the exercises as they go, some will zoom through in one sitting, and others will read sections in a random order. Therefore, the following questions don't have to be answered all at once or in any particular order. You may like to write down your answers in a journal, answer them in your head or discuss them with others. Use these questions to help you reflect on your experience and the things you've learned in order to support your growing sexual confidence.

Messages I received from others about sex and masturbation when growing up:

The messages I choose to accept now:

The messages I choose to reject now:

My plan for working through any psychological challenges:

My vision for myself sexually:

The positive effects of masturbation for me:

The story lines/fantasies/memories I find sexually arousing:

The senses that stand out the most for me in fantasies are: Visual, Smell, Sound, Taste, Touch (circle the key senses)

My arousal accelerators and turn-ons are:

My arousal brakes and turn-offs are:

The ways I set the scene for masturbating:

The music, if any, that helps me get aroused:

The parts of my body that feel especially sensitive sexually:

My favorite masturbation techniques:

My favorite masturbation positions:

Things I am going to explore to develop new neural pathways to orgasm:

How preference of direct or indirect clitoral stimulation varies during stages of arousal for me:

The effect of penetration on my arousal:

The effect of penetration during an orgasm:

My preferences for internal stimulation are:

My preferences for external stimulation are:

My response to edging:

Ways in which I am going to use mindfulness and meditation to boost my sexual experiences:

My favorite sex toys (and how I enjoy using them):

Things a sexual partner would benefit from knowing about my sexual preferences:

Three things I can do to loosen up the routine of sex:

Easy and/or fun ways I can exercise and move my body more during the day:

A simple change to make my diet more anti-inflammatory and sex-healthy:

The key things I learned from this book:

Something sexual I would still like to try:

5 things I love about my sexuality:

2. Useful resources and websites

OMGYes – Learn and practice masturbation techniques digitally using your finger and a smart phone screen.
Also discover more from interviews, research and women showing you how to do their favorite techniques. This is a website dedicated to education and research. Presented in an open, sex positive way. www.OMGyes.com

Labia Libraries – Understanding there is a wide variety of labia can help with body acceptance. There is no 'normal'. www.Labialibrary.org.au and http://www.hildeatalanta.com/thevulvagallery

Normal Vagina Smells – Get the low down on healthy vagina smells as well as when to seek treatment. https://www.healthline.com/health/womens-health/vagina-smells#8

Orgasm Sound Library – Listen to female orgasms and watch them be turned into artistic visuals. www.orgasmsoundlibrary.com/#gallery

Feminist Porn Guide – When searching for porn, I encourage you to support ethically made, feminist porn for reasons of actor safety and compensation. Be aware that the term 'porn for women' on mainstream free websites is often just used as a marketing tool and doesn't guarantee ethically produced videos.

https://feministporn.org/ run by the creator of the site Bright Desire provides information to further understand feminist porn along with extensive lists of recommended websites.

Accurate and up to date online sexual health resources – Two websites created and run by Myrtle Wilhite, MD, and Ellen Barnard, MSSW with free information on sexual health including downloadable brochures. The Femani website is about sexual health only, whereas the Sexuality Resources website also has information on sexual pleasure.

http://www.sexualityresources.com and http://femaniwellness.com

TEDx talks about the body and masturbation – TEDx has a wide range of inspiring masturbation, body acceptance and sex related videos available online or on the TEDx app. Some of my favorites include:

Masturbation is the New Meditation by Keeley Olivia: https://www.youtube.com/watch?v=BUOzUTXFlQA

A Motion for Masturbation – The Naked Truth. Jane Langton: https://www.youtube.com/watch?v=ZvSJE9n0GfA

The Vagina Whisperer by Tami Lynn Kent: https://www.youtube.com/watch?v=rK_P0UmpYd8

Performance Anxiety – It's Not Just for Men by Claudia Six, PhD: https://www.youtube.com/watch?v=mIxRPWHFWIM

Every Body is a Treasure by Mandi Lynn: https://www.youtube.com/watch?v=TGIIbuDsQBg

The Truth about Unwanted Arousal by Emily Nagoski: https://www.ted.com/talks/emily_nagoski_the_truth_about_u nwanted_arousal/up-next?language=en

Masturbation and orgasm education – Betty Dodson & Carlin Ross: Better Orgasms. Better World. Legendary sex educator and pro-sex feminist Betty and collaborator Carlin provide valuable sex education with their articles, videos, podcasts and workshops. If you want to watch videos demonstrating step-by-step methods of how to orgasm and getting comfortable with your vulva, this is your site. https://dodsonandross.com/

3. Conclusion

By the time you are reading this, you will hopefully have learned a lot and feel excited about continuing to play with your new ideas and awakening more and more of your sexual potential.

For me, it has been important to find my own way of experiencing and exploring my sexuality. It wasn't a one-off moment, but continues to be an ongoing learning process that changes and evolves with time. I have found the experience of self-pleasuring to be one that is fulfilling not only in terms of the obvious sexual enjoyment but also because of the learning and acceptance of my body, my individuality and my spirituality. It has benefited me and the relationship I have with my husband – both the sexual and emotional connection that we share. On another level, I know from the research that it is also very good for my health in numerous ways.

You may be wondering what next steps you can take from here – besides the obvious answer of putting aside some time on a regular basis to explore and pleasure yourself. It's really up to you, but what I would urge you to do is continue your learning and exploration of the topic of sex and sexuality. Sexuality is not something reserved for the days of our youth. We can enjoy elements of sexuality right up until our last breath. However, in order to do so, we have to decide to make it a priority, to value it as something we want to continue to experience and enjoy.

So get reading. There are thousands of books out there on the topic as well as websites, blogs, online articles, podcasts and videos – each with unique insights and information to expand your understanding. Additionally there are courses where you can immerse yourself in deepening experiences such as Tantra or mindfulness or women's sensuality. To feed your imagination and fantasies, you could explore sexually arousing stories and erotica as well as ethically produced pornography. Visiting a sex shop is another option, which no longer automatically means going to a seedy shop in an alleyway. Many sex shops have become much more respectable looking and if you are still uncomfortable about visiting in person, then find one online – you can then search through the various items in the privacy of your own home.

But don't get too caught up in the process, just start in any even small way and enjoy the journey – your individual journey. I wish you all the best of luck and hope that you too experience a sexual awakening that benefits you in more ways than you can even begin to imagine.

Also, thank you for reading this book. I know it's not a topic typically talked about around the coffee table but maybe you know of someone else who might benefit from exploring their sexuality as well – feel free to tell them about this book and the things you've learned. Who knows what interesting stories and sisterhood connection doing that might lead to!

I would love to hear about your journey and what works and has worked for you. I'm also happy for you to contact me with any questions you may have or with ideas with regards to how I could improve this book. Also remember you can give me a review online where you purchased this book. I'm sure other women will appreciate your honest opinion.

You can get in touch with me by sending an email to maree@nwow.co.nz or you can visit my website to find out more about what I do: www.nwow.co.nz

I wish you all the best in your journey!

Warm regards,

Maree Stachel-Williamson

REFERENCES

Auteri, S. (2014, May). The history of sensate focus, and how we self educate when it comes to evolving therapeutic techniques. AASECT. https://www.aasect.org/history-sensate-focus-and-how-we-self-educate-when-it-comes-evolving-therapeutic-techniques

Barnard, E., Wilhite, M. (n.d.). Vaginal renewal TM. A Woman's Touch: Sexuality Resource Center. https://sexualityresources.com/ask-dr-myrtle/womens-issues-and-sexual-problems/vaginal-renewal-tm

Bartlik, B.D., Kolzet, J.A., Ahmad, N., Parveen, T. & Alvi, S. (2010). Female sexual health. In Legato, J. (Ed.), Principles of gender-specific medicine (pp. 400-407). Elsevier Inc.

Bennet, L. & Holczer, G. (2010). Finding and revealing your sexual self: A guide to communicating about sex. Rowman & Littlefielld Publishers Inc.

Berman, L. (2008). The sex bible: Your bedside guide to a lifetime of sexual satisfaction. Dorling Kindersley Ltd.

Buehler S. PsyD, CST-S (n.d.). Practitioner resources

to accompany: What every mental health professional needs to know about sex. (2nd ed.). Springer Publishing Company, LLC.

Bijoux Indiscrets. (n.d.). Orgasm library of real sounds. https://orgasmsoundlibrary.com/#gallery

Blake, C. (2010). The joy of mindful sex: Be in the moment and enrich your lovemaking. Leaping Hare Press.

Bortz II, W.M., & Stickrod, R. (2010). The roadmap to 100: The breakthrough science of living a long and healthy life. Palgrave Macmillan.

Chan, K.B.K. (2013, January 31). Jam [Video]. YouTube. https://www.youtube.com/watch?v=bgd3m-x46JU

Chia, M., & Abrams, D. (2010). The multi-orgasmic man: Sexual secrets every man should know. HarperCollins Publishers Inc.

Chia, M., & Carlton Abrams, R. (2010). The multi-orgasmic woman: Sexual secrets every woman should know. HarperCollins Publishers Inc.

Comfort, A., & Quilliam, S. (2008). The new joy of sex. Octopus Publishing Group Ltd.

Cornell Health. (2019, 18 October). Sensate focus. https://health.cornell.edu/sites/health/files/pdf-library/sensate-focus.pdf

Current pleasures. (n.d.) Safety. https://www.currentpleasures.com/pages/instructions-safety

Dangerous Lilly (2018, April 03). Lelo Sona Cruise Review. Dangerous Lilly. http://dangerouslilly.com/2018/04/lelo-sona-cruise-review/

Dee, J. (2016, August 30). The dual control model –
Why you sometimes can't get in the mood for sex.
Uncovering Intimacy.
https://www.uncoveringintimacy.com/dual-control-
model-sometimes-cant-get-mood-sex/

Dubberly, E. (2014). Garden of desires: The evolution of
women's sexual fantasies. Ebury Publishing.

Fletcher, J. (2019, October 29). What to know about
Ben Wa balls. Medical News Today.
https://www.medicalnewstoday.com/articles/326832.php

Flynn, M.G., Mc Farlin, B.K. & Markofski, M.M.
(2007 May-June). The anti-inflammatory actions of
exercise training. American Journal of Lifestyle
Medicine. 1 (3): 220-235   doi:
10.1177/1559827607300283

Friday, N. (2008). My secret garden. Simon & Schuster.

Friday, N. (1993). Women on top. Arrow Books Ltd.

Greger, M. (2017, April 5). Best foods to improve sexual
function [Video]. NutritionFacts.org.
https://nutritionfacts.org/video/best-foods-to-improve-
sexual-function/

Gusakova, S. Conley, T. D., Piemonte, J. L., Matsick, J.
L. (2019). The role of women's orgasm goal pursuit in
women's orgasm occurrence. Personality and Individual
Differences. http://doi.org/10.1016/j.paid.2019.10628

Inkeles, G., & Todris, M. (1977). The art of sensual
massage. (Mandala ed.). Unwin Paperbacks.

Janssen, E., & Bancroft, J. (2006). The dual control
model: The role of sexual inhibition & excitation in
sexual arousal and behavior. In Janssen, E. (Ed.), The

psychophysiology of sex.   Indiana University Press. https://www.kinseyinstitute.org/pdf/Janssen_Bancroft_2 006.pdf

Jewell, T. (2018). Everything you need to know about the refractory period. Healthline. https://www.healthline.com/health/healthy-sex/refractory-period

Kauppi, M. (2017, December 5). Are vibrators habit-forming? Institute for Relational Intimacy. https://instituteforrelationalintimacy.com/are-vibrators-habit-forming/

Kauppi, M. (2019). Dual control model of arousal. In Assessing & Treating Sex Issues in Psychotherapy: 2019 [Video Transcript]. Institute for Relational Intimacy.

Kauppi, M. (2019). Module 05: Pelvic Anatomy. In Assessing & Treating Sex Issues in Psychotherapy: 2019 [Class lecture slides]. Institute for Relational Intimacy.

Kauppi, M. (2019). Module 08: Physiology of Arousal. In Assessing & Treating Sex Issues in Psychotherapy: 2019 [Class lecture slides]. Institute for Relational Intimacy.

Kermani, K. Dr. (1996). Autogenic training: The effective holistic way to better health. Profile Books Ltd.

Komisaruk, B.R., Beyer-Flores, C., & Whipple, B. (2006) The science of orgasm. (1st ed.). Johns Hopkins University Press.

Korff, J. and James H. Geer. (1983). The relationship between sexual arousal experience and genital response. Psychophysiology, 20(2), 121-127

Lehmiller, J. (2020, Mar/Apr) The seven most common sexual fantasies. *Psychology Today, 53 (2)*, 28-31.

Literotica. (n.d.) Stories.
https://www.literotica.com/stories/

Loofbourow, L. (2018, January 25). The female price of male pleasure. The Week.
http://theweek.com/articles/749978/female-price-male-pleasure

Lynn, M. TEDxWellington. (2019, August 30). Every body is a treasure [Video]. YouTube.
https://www.youtube.com/watch?v=TGIIbuDsQBg

Maltz, W. (2012). The sexual healing journey: A guide for survivors of sexual abuse. HarperCollins Publishers Inc.

Masters, W.H., Johnson, V.E., & Kolodny, R.C. (1986). Masters and Johnson on sex and human loving. Little, Brown and Company Inc.

McBurney, L. (2013, August). Is masturbation a sin? Todays Christian Woman.
http://www.todayschristianwoman.com/articles/2013/august/is-masturbation-sin.html

McCarthy, B., & McCarthy, E. (2003). Rekindling desire: A step-by-step program to help low-sex and no-sex marriages. Brunner Routledge.

Meiller, C., & Hargons, C. N. (2019). It's happiness and relief and release: Exploring masturbation among bisexual and queer women. Journal of Counseling Sexology & Sexual Wellness: Research, Practice, and Education, 1 (1), 6. https://doi.org/10.34296/01011009

Michigan Medicine. (n.d.). Mind-body wellness. University of Michigan.
https://www.uofmhealth.org/health-library/mente

Netsafe. (2020, July 14). Understanding nudes and sexting. https://www.netsafe.org.nz/sexting/

Obos Anatomy & Menstruation Contributors. (2014, March 28). Self-exam: Vulva and vagina. Our Bodies Ourselves. https://www.ourbodiesourselves.org/book-excerpts/health-article/self-exam-vulva-vagina/

Oredsson, E. (2015, October 31). Art history 101: The female nude. How To Talk About Art History: It's Easier Than It Seems. http://www.howtotalkaboutarthistory.com/art-history-101/art-history-101-the-female-nude-nsfw/

O'Reilly, J. (2010, September 1). A is for A-spot – Can you find it? Sex with Dr. Jess. https://www.sexwithdrjess.com/2010/09/a-is-for-a-spot-can-you-find-it/

Orwig, J. (2014, November 8). Here's what women fantasize about the most. Business Insider Australia. https://www.businessinsider.com.au/what-women-fantasize-about-2014-11?r=US&IR=T

Poulsen, F.O., Busby, D.M., & Galovan, A.M. (2013). Pornography use: who uses it and how it is associated with couple outcomes. Journal of Sex Research. *50*(1), 72–83. https://doi.org/10.1080/00224499.2011.648027

Psychology Today. (n.d.). Hypersexuality. https://www.psychologytoday.com/nz/conditions/hypersexuality-sex-addiction

Regehr, R. (2015, July 8). How the history of pubic hair removal exposes society's illusions about your body. Everyday Feminism. https://everydayfeminism.com/2015/07/history-pubic-hair/

Richmond, R.L. Ph.D. (n.d). Autogenics training. A Guide to Psychology and its Practice. http://www.guidetopsychology.com/autogen.htm

Staff, H. (2009, January 4). Women's top 10 sexual

fantasies. HealthyPlace.
https://www.healthyplace.com/sex/psychology-of-sex/womens-top-ten-sexual-fantasies

Steelsmith, L., & Steelsmith, A. (2012). Great sex naturally: Every woman's guide to enhancing her sexuality through the secrets of natural medicine. Hay House, Inc.

Stephenson-Connolly, P. (2011). Sex life: How our sexual experiences define who we are. Vermilion.

Summers, J. (2001, November 1). What is ghost fucking? Joanne's sex machine and sex toy reviews. https://www.sexmachinereviews.co.uk/estim-electrosex/e-stim-faq/electrode-faq/what-is-ghost-fucking.html

The Pamela Madsen [@thepamelamadsen]. (2019, July 15). Things a 93 year old woman says on a sexuality retreat. [Photograph]. Instagram. https://www.instagram.com/p/Bz6d9XYBVTl/?igshid=1pe4cme9406k0

The Pamela Madsen [@thepamelamadsen]. (2019, December 15). Women learn about sex through the eyes of the world around them. [Photograph]. Instagram. https://www.instagram.com/p/B6EQCk5B7ct/?igshid=qbxkgqh3hqtu

Tigar, L. (n.d.). How to watch porn safely: All the pro tips you need to watch xxx movies online safely. Ask Men. https://uk.askmen.com/sex/sex_tips/how-to-watch-porn-safely.html

UCLA Health. Pelvic floor rehabilitation. Retrieved 2018, February 9 from http://urology.ucla.edu/pelvic-floor-rehabilitation

Valdez, N.J. (2011) Vitamin O: Why orgasms are vital to a woman's health and happiness, and how to have them every time. Skyhorse Publishing Ltd.

Westheimer, R., Grunebaum, A. & Lehu, P. (2012). Sexually speaking: What every woman needs to know about sexual health. John Wiley & Sons, Inc.

Zobel, H. (2019, October 21). Billie Eilish on the best way to fight stress. Spiegel International. https://www.spiegel.de/international/zeitgeist/billie-eilish-talks-about-depression-and-how-she-copes-with-stress-a-1292606.html

ABOUT THE AUTHOR

Maree Stachel-Williamson is a therapist based in New Zealand. In her books, she aims to help others with topics and issues that have been important in her own life as well as those that regularly come up for her clients. Honest and to the point, she shares her expertise with the aim of empowering people to find solutions that work for them. www.nwow.co.nz

Maree has a diverse training background, which includes NLP (Neuro-Linguistic Programming), Person-Centered Counseling, EFT (Emotional Freedom Techniques), Mindfulness Based Stress Reduction (MBSR), Family and Structural Constellation Work, Ericksonian and Clinical Hypnotherapy, Time-Line Therapy ™, Clean Language, Assessing and Treating Sex Issues in Psychotherapy and TFH Kinesiology (Touch for Health).

Other e-books by Maree available for purchase online:

– Stop Painful Sex: Healing Vaginismus – A Step by Step Guide

– The Baby Dilemma: How to Decide

Printed in Great Britain
by Amazon

50413598R00139